WHAT MINISTERS CAN'T LEARN IN SEMINARY

WHAT MINISTERS CAN'T LEARN IN SEMINARY

A SURVIVAL MANUAL for the PARISH MINISTRY

R. ROBERT CUENI

ABINGDON PRESS

Nashville

WHAT MINISTERS CAN'T LEARN IN SEMINARY
A SURVIVAL MANUAL FOR THE PARISH MINISTRY

Copyright © 1988 by Abingdon Press

This book is printed on acid-free paper.

Library of Congress Cataloging-in-Publication Data
Cueni, R. Robert.
    What ministers can't learn in seminary: a survival manual for the parish ministry/R. Robert Cueni.
        p. cm.
    Includes bibliographical references.
    ISBN 0-687-44652-X (pbk.: alk. paper)
    1. Pastoral theology. 2. Clergy—Office. I. Title.
BV4011.C84   1988   88-6325
253—dc19   CIP

Scripture quotations unless otherwise noted are from the Revised Standard Version of the Bible, copyrighted 1946, 1952, 1971 by the Division of Christian Education of the National Council of the Churches of Christ in the U.S.A., and used by permission.

Those noted NEB are from The New English Bible. © The Delegates of the Oxford University Press and the Syndics of the Cambridge University Press 1961, 1970. Reprinted by permission.

Those designated GNB are from the Good News Bible—Old Testament: Copyright © American Bible Society 1976; New Testament: Copyright © American Bible Society 1966, 1971, 1976.

Manufactured by the Parthenon Press at
Nashville, Tennessee, United States of America

TO

Linda, my partner in ministry and life

ACKNOWLEDGMENTS

Ŧ

I have been very fortunate. Some outstanding people have shown me the ways of ministry. Their lessons and examples have saved me the pain of learning everything by trial and error. While not possible to name everyone who had a part in shaping my ministry and this book, I would like to thank a few.

Raymond Gaylord, pastor of Cascade Christian Church, Grand Rapids, Michigan, has been my spiritual father in ministry. He saw my possibilities, offered me a position on his staff, pushed me toward seminary, and has been my mentor for over twenty years. Had he not given me the initial shove, I might never have started down this road. The Disciples of Christ congregations I have served since then in Springport and Bedford, Indiana, Petoskey, Michigan, and Bloomington, Illinois, shaped me by their love and contributed to this book by providing many illustrations.

Illinois colleagues Herb Knudsen and Gail Bell were invaluable in helping me think through what I wanted to write. Herb Miller, Lubbock, Texas, gave indispensable technical advice and personal encouragement. Steve Dungan's editing skills helped me at just the right time, and Debbie Stumm provided outstanding secretarial services.

I am, of course, always thankful for Linda, my wife of twenty-five years, who encouraged me through rewrite after rewrite. Finally, I give thanks to my daughters, Karen and Colleen. On those Sundays when the worship service does not seem to fall together, they lift my spirits and cause me to rejoice that I decided to spend my life in pastoral ministry. All they need do is comment, "Daddy, when we see you in the pulpit, it makes us so proud."

CONTENTS

𝕱

INTRODUCTION

Few occupations offer the satisfaction potential that the pastoral ministry does. The daily routine provides a variety of experiences, requires multiple skills, tests the limits of creativity, and permits great freedom. What a delightful way to spend your life's energy. For most clergy, living with and serving God's people gives them more than it takes.

One should never assume, however, that competence in ministry comes naturally or quickly. The satisfaction resulting from effectively performing pastoral duties is not automatically bestowed with every seminary diploma. It blossoms from skills that are only tiny buds at graduation time. Conversations, particularly among less experienced clergy, reveal widespread dissatisfaction. Rather than rejoicing in their calling, they often complain about the parish, the parishioners, the pay, and the other problems of being a local church pastor. Rather than feeling confident about what they do, they feel overwhelmed. Many have not discovered how to perform the varied responsibilities of pastoral ministry in personally and professionally fulfilling ways.

Fortunately, however, most eventually learn what it takes to make the most of pastoral ministry. A study conducted by the Midwest Career Development Center revealed that more than three out of four experienced parish ministers are satisfied.[1] In a random sample poll, 84 percent reported that they enjoyed their work "most of the time" or "all of the time." The more experienced the pastor, however, the higher the sense of satisfaction and the firmer the sense of professional identity—not to mention enhanced effectiveness that comes with years of experience. Significantly, the study also revealed that younger pastors are not as happy at what they do. They have lower levels of work satisfaction and a higher sense of personal and professional loneliness. Whereas more experienced clergy report fulfillment in ministry, younger clergy report being overwhelmed by the complexities of the pastoral role.

Veteran clergy apparently know what it takes. The experience of serving as a local church pastor continues the education that began in seminary. The lessons gained through practical experience make it possible to move from overwhelmed to confident and from miserable to satisfied.

Although the majority of clergy accomplish this crucial transition, they do it by the process of trial

---

1. Study quoted in *The Christian Ministry*, May, 1986, p. 21. Details available from Midwest Career Development Center, Westchester, Illinois, L. Ronald Brushwyler.

and error. For years they practice ministry as the walking wounded. Eventually they learn from shooting themselves in the foot and begin to practice local church ministry in more satisfying ways. In hopes of shortcutting some of the pain inherent to that haphazard process, this book outlines some key principles for thinking about and doing ministry that lead to pastoral satisfaction.

CANOEING AND THE PASTORAL MINISTRY

A newly ordained minister and his young wife underwent the first severe test of the stability of their marriage when they accompanied the Young Couple's Sunday School Class on a day-long canoe trip. She had never been in a canoe. His experience was limited to a distant memory of a quiet lake at Boy Scout Camp. Neither of them were prepared for six hours on the rock infested, logjammed, and constantly swirling waters of an angry river.

Since the brochure said "Beginner's Stream," they did not worry. They assumed canoeing was like the boat trip at the amusement park. No skill required. Just get on and ride. They had gone only fifty feet from the dock when the canoe turned 180 degrees. They floated backward for another twenty feet before they hit a log and overturned in two feet of rushing water. They spent the next hour moving from shoreline to shoreline, uprighting the canoe from numerous spills, expending an enormous amount of energy trying to steer a craft that seemed to defy all known laws of navigation and heatedly debating the intelligence of the one to whom they had pledged "to love, honor and cherish until death do us part" just a few months before. By the end of the first hour, they concluded canoeing was, at best, the second leading cause of divorce in America or, at worst, usually fatal. Certainly they lost all hope that they could ever become competent canoeists or that there could ever be anything enjoyable about the experience.

During the second hour, they began to discover some basic principles of canoeing. Quite by accident, they learned how to control the canoe by paddling faster than the stream's current. Eventually not only could they keep the canoe going in a straight line, but they could also steer it in the direction they wanted it to go. They even managed to miss an occasional rock. Being wet became the accepted standard and they prepared for it. Rather than always fighting the strength of the current, they learned to cooperate with it.

By the end of the day, canoeing became for them downright enjoyable. What started out being misery ended up being a delight. The difference was learning and applying a few simple rules. Today, canoeing ranks as a favorite family outing. They still take time to refresh their memories on the principles for operating this strange craft. Once accomplished, however, their ability to navigate even a difficult stream makes the outing highly enjoyable.

The skills needed in canoeing and pastoral ministry do not come naturally. Certain principles must be learned. Even without knowing what to do, one can attempt to canoe or to serve as a pastoral minister. However, enjoyment comes only to those who learn to apply the principles, and, generally speaking, only frustration comes to those who do not. In both cases, simply knowing the rules does not ensure satisfaction. One can be an excellent canoeist and still not care for it. The same is true for the pastorate. Knowing how to do it only opens the possibility for satisfaction; it does not ensure it.

CHAPTER I

SEMINARY DIFFERS FROM
THE LOCAL PARISH

Pulpit giant Howard Crosby preached at New York's Fourth Avenue Presbyterian Church from 1863 until his death in 1891. In 1880 he delivered the prestigious Lyman Beecher Lectures at Yale. His topic, "The Christian Preacher," addressed the practical skills of parish ministry. In making his point, Crosby strenuously objected to the cloistered life of the typical seminary experience in the nineteenth century. The "ordinary minister comes out of seminary an imbecile," the great preacher declared. He went on to explain. A minister "may be a good scholar, an able reasoner, a devoted servant of God, but his place is still in the seminary, not in the seething cauldron of the world."[1]

In the past century seminary education has changed significantly. Seminary curricula have overcome the problems of cloistering by exposing students to more than academic disciplines. Seminaries usually require practical experience in local congregations. Most seminaries even offer the course equivalent of M-604: Seething Cauldron of the World.

Crosby's conclusion that the ministers come out of seminary unprepared for front-line parish duty, however, still deserves consideration. Because the seminary cannot be equated to life in the parish, the new seminary graduate must undergo a significant transition before he or she can enjoy the blessings of ministry. College prepares people to study in college. Seminary prepares people to study in seminary. The minister must still learn to apply what these institutions teach. Only experience empowers this transition from theory to practical application.

When a family drove from northern Michigan to San Francisco, they prepared carefully. Because it was their first trip, they carried in the front seat of the car an enormous plastic bag filled with maps and brochures. They had information on everything from side roads to rest rooms to the tourist attractions that crowded their planned route of over two thousand miles.

---

1. Edgar DeWitt Jones, *The Royalty of the Pulpit* (New York: Harper & Brothers, 1951), p. 38.

At one point, the father flipped the "AAA Trip Tic" to the stretch of road between Buffalo, Wyoming and Ten Sleep, Wyoming. This page looked basically the same as every other page in the itinerary. It showed a crooked black line across a white page. In the margin, he noted the altitude went from 2,000 feet above sea level to 7,000 feet and back to 2,000 and correctly reasoned, "We are going to cross a range of the Rocky Mountains." He had watched Marlin Perkins and Walt Disney films about the Rockies. He had heard fellow flatlanders talk about hairpin turns, sheer cliffs, and no guard rails. Intellectually, he was fully aware of the nature of a road that goes over a mountain.

He quickly discovered that his knowledge of the Rocky Mountains did not prepare him for reality. His slight fear of heights greatly intensified to make it the most terrifying journey of his life. All the information gathered about mountains did not prepare him for the experience. Maps of mountains differ significantly from driving over them.

Seminary is three years of reading, lectures, discussions, and occasional weekend forays into the local church. This prepares the seminarian for a pastorate in the same way reading a map prepared the travelers for driving over a mountain.

Seminaries frequently receive the blame for this problem. Graduate theological education even seems open to the criticism. A typical seminary faculty has ten academicians for every person with fifteen to twenty years of solid pastoral experience. Seminary requirements are heavy on theology and church history and light on pastoral administration. The local church pastor's day-to-day routine may require learning multiple techniques for getting a functional committee functioning, but the seminary spends much more time on the Council of Nicea. This critical bit of history has little practical application in mediating a church fight. For reasons as these, seminaries are frequently easy targets for criticism by local pastors and lay leaders.

The criticism must be dismissed as unfair. Seminary cannot be equated to trade school. If Susie wants to be an auto mechanic, she can buy a set of tools and enroll in a mechanic course to learn how to use them. The trade school will instruct her in the use of tools she can purchase in a hardware store.

If Susie wants to be a minister, she cannot purchase the tools in a store. A seminary education provides them. Only through the experience of working in a local church and by taking carefully selected continuing education events can she develop the skills to use the tools provided by the initial seminary experience.

Attempts to make the basic seminary degree comparable to a trade school education by providing more training in the practical aspects of ministry are futile. One must possess the tools of the trade before one can learn to use them. Additionally, seminary studies already include practical lessons, but seminarians cannot yet appreciate their significance. Knowledge must be empowered by experience. Although maps and seminaries are needed, they differ significantly from mountains and local churches.

NO PLACE TO COPY ONE'S TEACHERS

Do not become confused, misinterpret the data, and conclude that pastorates are extensions of academia. Seminary differs greatly from the experience of local church pastorates. These differences include everything from the experienced rhythm of daily life, to the fact that there are no mandatory readings, to the amount of time one can devote to personal study.

The local church pastor typically believes that college and seminary professors have glorious ministries. The professor is imagined ministering only to highly motivated students rather than to an uninterested congregation. Rather than finding time only to read for sermon illustrations, the professor is thought perpetually curled up with a book in the corner of the study. Rather than racing from committee meeting to committee meeting, the local church pastor believes the academic spends long hours each day contemplating the personalities of those who voted on early church creeds. No wonder clergy frequently envy their professors. They spend most waking moments pursuing truth and contemplating the meaning of life.

The pastor who models his or her ministry on this inaccurate perception of the academic life will be frustrated in the local church as well as disillusioned by the reality of the day-to-day routine of the academic. Acting as if the pastor should be nothing more than the Resident Intellectual Only for Addressing Ontological Concerns gives an entirely new meaning to the expression "living under stress."

A senior minister was asked to screen candidates for an associate minister's position. He wanted the committee to talk with a young man who was completing a Ph.D. at a seminary affiliated with a prestigious university. He told the committee, "Due to the shortage of teaching jobs, he is willing to hold an open mind on our position of associate minister." Far from being impressed by his credentials, the committee members' attitude was summarized by a fellow who said, "And we will try to keep an open mind about his education and not hold it against him."

This was not a group of anti-intellectuals. The church was in a college community. Many members held Ph.D. degrees themselves. The congregation simply had had experience with clergy who attempted to practice parish ministry as an extension of academia.

MORE BOREDOM THAN EXCITEMENT

Seminary can be a satisfying time. The lectures, the fellowship of the gathered community, and even the term papers can make seminary a continual intellectual and spiritual high.

From that pinnacle, the first pastorate can easily become a downer. It can be incredibly difficult to make the adjustment. After the excitement of school, many new pastors miss everything from the intellectual ferment to the term paper deadlines.

Mary and Joseph may have experienced the same adjustment. The birth of Jesus was accompanied by a choir of angels singing praises to the Child. The young couple busied themselves greeting shepherds. The Magi brought expensive gifts and told stories of the star they followed. For a peasant couple from the northern hill country, this was pretty exciting stuff.

Then the angelic chorus fell silent. The shepherds left to find their wandering sheep. The Magi packed the camel saddlebags and headed home. In the quiet left behind, Mary and Joseph must have heard the crying of the baby Jesus. He needed to be fed and changed. The daily grind of caring for an infant's every need stretched endlessly before them. The holy couple must have looked at one another and thought, "You have got to be kidding! This is it, no more angels, shepherds, or wise men?"

The first pastorate has the same effect. It usually involves a move from an urban seminary campus to a small town, from a multitude of friends to a crowd of strangers, from an abundance of theologically trained colleagues to a community where only an occasional person knows the name Paul Tillich. Seminary life was familiar. One knew what was expected and how one would be evaluated in meeting those expectations. The questions of the first pastorate are unavoidable: What am I supposed to be doing? and Will I be able to do it well?

At least initially, local church ministry is boring when compared to student life. However, some intentional reworking of priorities and expectations facilitates the transition. Mary and Joseph must have gone through the same process. Like most parents, the holy couple probably told stories of how the joys of raising Jesus were, in the long run, far more rewarding than the excitement at his birth. Similarly, there are significant rewards in the daily routine whereby the pastor shares the joys, pains, and turning points of an entire congregation of the people of God.

ISSUES ARE USUALLY COMPLEX

Serious problems seldom, if ever, have simple resolutions. No topic can be exhausted in a ten-page term paper. Contrary to the impression left by television, the most violent crimes cannot be solved in a half-hour mystery. Significant social problems cannot be analyzed in a one-hour documentary. Contrary to the resolutions passed by most denominational assemblies, the Christian position on social and ethical issues cannot be determined by a majority of those present who vote on a statement with three "whereas" clauses and one "therefore, let it be resolved."

An older rabbi had a reputation of being an outstanding marriage counselor. The seminary student observing his counseling technique was disappointed. "Rabbi, I am dumbfounded," the rabbinical student said. "When Mrs. Birnbaum came to you complaining about her husband, you listened. When she finished, you told her 'I agree with you Mrs. Birnbaum, your husband is impossible and you are doing everything expected of a wife.' This afternoon, Mr. Birnbaum came to see you and complained about his wife. You listened and told him, 'Mr. Birnbaum, you are right. You are married to an impossible woman. You are doing everything expected of a husband.' "

"That is ridiculous," the young man complained to the old rabbi. "You told them both they were doing fine and their spouse was to blame. Either the husband or the wife has to be doing something wrong. They both cannot be totally right and both totally wrong!"

The rabbi thought about the accusation for a few moments as he stroked his beard. "You know, my son," the wise old fellow finally said, "You are right. *You* are right."

Ministers must be compassionate listeners. Opening their minds to the views of others leads them to see a bit of truth in nearly every opinion. It may be a partial or twisted truth, but still a bit of truth. The pastor who remains open to what others think, feel, and say frequently feels like the rabbi caught between the Birnbaums.

Although it can be frustrating to see both sides of an issue, that ability is required for ministry. The person who finds it necessary to take a stand on every issue and give no quarter to those who differ has a narrow view of truth and will find local church ministry uncomfortable rather than satisfying.

SATISFACTION IN THE UNFINISHED

Seminary has a marvelous rhythm. The semester begins, builds to a peak, winds down with exams and term papers, then dies, only to be resurrected as a new semester with new courses. This provides a sense of completeness. A grade will be given, study set aside, and the text deposited on the bookshelf. When the cycle has been repeated often enough, graduation comes. Educational satisfaction comes in working within this cycle.

Although different, parish life has a definite rhythm. It works its way through the passing weeks and seasons of the church year. Seldom, however, does one have the experience of wrapping it up and never being forced to think about it again. Rather than mastering an issue and setting it aside for a new challenge, parish life presents the same problems over and over. Satisfaction in ministry must be found without the sense of completion that seminary offered.

Laity sometimes inquire about the nature of ministry. They assume it is interesting to help people work through their problems. How disappointing to discover most problems are routine. After listening to the first few, mediating extramarital affairs can be as routine as shoveling snow and nearly as exhausting. Helping the family decide the time for grandma to enter the nursing home never has a Stephen King twist. Events hurting families seldom suggest plots for new television series. The same problems and discussions happen over and over. The person who waits for satisfaction to come after finishing a job and getting on to something new will be frustrated in the pastorate.

The rewards of ministry come by being with people during the tough times. A problem may occasionally be solved. A word of encouragement will be offered. Perhaps the pastor may even be thanked for saying something helpful. These rewards come from being present at the right time as an instrument of God's love. While not spectacular, they can be satisfying.

MINISTRY IS HARD WORK

On occasion someone wanders into the pastorate with a fatal misunderstanding. He/she assumes ministry in the local church is easy. Perhaps such a person takes too seriously the coffee shop chatter about "Preacher, I envy you. I would sure enjoy a job where I could work just one day a week and be done by noon."

Whatever the source of this erroneous notion, effective pastoral ministry precludes the possibility of personal laziness. If one expects to experience satisfaction, he/she must be willing to exert enormous effort. The job description of a local pastor does not promise forty-hour weeks, evenings free, and never a phone call after 9:00 P.M. The hours are long and the emergencies frequent. The funerals often come on the day set aside for a family activity.

Although he/she need not become a workaholic, effective ministry demands the mastering of time management. Only then can ample opportunity be found for family, vacation, and a regular schedule. It cannot be overemphasized, that without disciplining one's time, the job will be overwhelming.

Unfortunately many laity make a good case that "our preacher is just plain lazy." The puritan strain in American history considers this a serious sin. When members of the congregation perceive such a flaw, they usually express their dissatisfaction publicly. This can result in ministerial mastication—the process by which the congregation chews the minister into little pieces.

Lazy ministers also bring misery upon themselves. It starts as a twinge of boredom but quickly degenerates to serious depression. How easily this happens! When individuals spend much of each day in inactivity, they will be bored. When boredom becomes a way of life, depression soon follows. Although hard work alone will not cure depression or guarantee a satisfying ministry, it does not hurt. In fact, just the willingness to exert effort opens possibilities closed to those who are not willing to put in a day's work for a day's pay.

Pastoral ministry will not be trouble free. Faith never promises that if you love the Lord, you will have health, wealth, and kids without cavities. Rather than being treated as royalty, a servant of

Christ's Church is frequently treated as the hired hand. In spite of being new creations in Christ, church members continue to act like sinners. Whether in ministry or not, life can be a struggle. Only the unrealistic expect it to be different. In the Master's parable, the rain falls on the house built on the rock as well as the house built on the sand. The house on the rock gets wet but avoids destruction. Such is the promise of faith. Life will not always be easy, but by a more disciplined faith, we shall survive the hard times.

REWARDS WILL NOT BE MONETARY

The message may not have gotten through during seminary that ministry does not pay well. Frequently the pay is poor. Most of the time, the minister attains financial comfort. On rare occasion, pay slightly exceeds the range of the comfortable.

In this profession, however, riches are best measured in meaningful relationships, long-term friendships, and the remembered opportunities for serving as an instrument of God's love. Unnecessary disappointment comes to those who expect monetary wealth.

OFF TO THE RIGHT START

The differences between seminary and parish life are significant. The more quickly these can be identified and integrated into the thought and action of the local church minister, the more quickly he/she will begin to experience the joys of the pastorate.

CHAPTER II

KEEP THE RELATIONSHIP HEALTHY

When John became minister of old First Church his predecessor offered some wise words of advice. "John, I served this congregation for twenty-seven years before I retired. Most of those years were wonderful. Some were not. The one lesson I want to pass on from my experience is this: If you love these people and they know it, they will forgive any error, overlook any shortcoming, and permit you to do your job about any way you choose. If, however, you even give them the impression you don't like or appreciate them, nothing you do will please them."

Performing ministry in a local congregation requires a relationship of mutual respect and caring between pastor and people. Within this covenant, God mediates the love, mercy, and power needed for daily life. Without a healthy bonding for pastoral care, one finds it extremely difficult, if not impossible, to minister. In addition, the minister's satisfaction depends on it.

Several factors determine whether a satisfying relationship develops. Obviously, the minister must be perceived as a trustworthy, credible, committed, and competent person. Ministers who break confidences, who do not seem to believe the gospel they preach, or who do not seem to know what they are doing, encounter serious problems establishing and maintaining trust.

More than professional competence and Christian commitment are required to develop a high quality relationship with the members. "Does the minister like me and respect my beliefs?" will be asked more frequently than, "Is our pastor well-versed in the realized eschatology of the Gospel of John?" In fact, whether the minister assesses the tenure in a given congregation as meaningful and satisfying may depend more on whether the pastor "liked" the people and the people "liked" the pastor than any other factor. Church members, as normal human beings, want to be loved, respected, and valued as well as to love, respect, and value the significant people in their lives, including the pastor. When a congregation has a positive relationship with the pastor, the ministry has the potential to be effective and satisfying.

A high quality of the pastor-congregation relationship also enhances the authority to do ministry. In the mind of the congregation, it takes more than ordination to make a minister. Congregations grant authority for ministry when they perceive the pastor not only as a competent, ordained professional and committed Christian, but as a trustworthy human being who respects, loves, and values the membership as fellow children of God. Where such a bonding exists, the possibility of effective and satisfying ministry escalates geometrically.

To establish and maintain a quality relationship with the congregation ranks as one of the pastoral minister's most demanding tasks. During the first few years with a congregation, more time may be spent building the relationship with the church folks than on any other task. Even when established, the relationship cannot be taken for granted. Relationship maintenance can be as important and as demanding as sermon preparation.

WAR IS NOT HEALTHY

Every church pastor's first priority should be to establish a relationship of trust and respect with the people. Every program, decision, and act of pastoral care depends on this bonding. Some well intentioned ministers make the mistake of putting other priorities before the relationships. This usually has disastrous results. Without a base of trust and respect, pastor and congregation come to act toward each other as enemies rather than friends. Unless defused, these hostilities will continue to escalate.

ɔmetimes mistakenly put other priorities
ablishing trust. In their most common
ɣ are false assumptions the pastor makes
about ministry or the congregation. When one of
these assumptions becomes the pastor's priority, the
relationship erodes. Before long, a battle begins in
the church. When congregational life resembles a
battlefield, the ministry cannot be effective and little
satisfaction comes to parson or parish.

Consider the following as church battles started
by well-intentioned ministers who acted on erroneous assumptions. Their first priority should have
been to develop the relationship between the
minister and congregation.

BATTLE #1

*Instead of working toward mutual respect, the pastor
sees the congregation as a problem to solve.*

Thirty-five-year-old Pastor Jim presently serves
his fifth congregation since seminary graduation
ten years ago. According to him, the other four
congregations had such serious problems that no
minister could have expected to stay long. Although
those ministries were difficult, he learned and grew
from each. When the opportunity came to serve this
larger congregation in a larger town, he believed he
was ready for the challenge.

After two months, his enthusiasm has dimin-
ished. He claims his predecessor was a terrible
administrator. The committee infrastructure and
program of the church are practically nonexistent.
Some people are angry at the former pastor. Others
grieve his departure. Jim's reconciling skills are
being tested to the limits by this congregation.

Apparently little, if anything, has been done with Christian nurture because the level of biblical and theological understanding is appalling. Jim believes this congregation has big problems.

Jim had hoped for things to be different. At each of his former charges he arrived to discover similar problems. He wonders if other clergy ever do the job they are called to do. Is he getting the reputation as a troubleshooter for problem churches? He has grown weary of always having to straighten things out. The task consumes his energy, and he burns out after a few years. He wants to believe that a better way exists. He does not want to repeat his three-year cycle at this church doing the work others should have done.

LESSON TO LEARN

Do not come to a new parish as a missionary to pagans.

Pastor Jim enters each new congregation assuming the parish has a serious problem he must solve. His preaching and education programs are established on the assumption that this parish has not heard the gospel. He assumes his predecessors knew little about administration. Therefore, he feels he must build the infrastructure of congregational life from the ground up.

Because he acts on this erroneous assumption, Jim's relationship with the people always gets off to a rocky start. He believes the people are a problem to solve rather than the children of God to love. Because he treats them as problems, they behave accordingly. Their response confirms Jim's assumptions about the troubled nature of every congregation he has served. Consequently, he accelerates the problem-solving methods that stiffen the congregation's resentment over Jim's treatment. Before long, Jim and the congregation are locked in an action-reaction pattern of relating. When called to another congregation, he reestablishes this same pattern of relating that eventually has the same results.

Even before arriving, Jim needs to call a truce with the congregation by altering some of the assumptions he makes about congregations and pastoral ministry. Local church pastors do not qualify as missionaries to pagans who have never heard the gospel. In each parish, the present pastor stands in line with those who have faithfully served since that congregation's establishment. Every previous minister made a contribution to the faith of the community. If Jim permits himself to be set free from assuming he must always be solving problems and plowing new ground, he will more than likely enjoy his tenure.

A pastor also gains much strength from recognizing that ministers are part of the ongoing community that extends back to Jerusalem on the day of Pentecost. Jim does not start fresh with each congregation. He builds on a foundation of faith laid centuries ago. Certainly, he will make a contribution. There will be strengths he can bring to the congregation that the previous ministers may not have had. He does not, however, carry the responsibility for saving every congregation from destruction.

When Jim permits himself to be set free of seeing congregations as problems to solve and himself their savior, he will be open to establishing more enjoyable relationships. His skills will then be appreciated. This will not happen, however, unless he seeks first to establish a relationship of trust and respect with the people.

BATTLE #2

Instead of working to establish mutual respect, the pastor decides to fight for power.

Before making a decision for ministry, Sue had a career in banking. As a branch manager she successfully managed people and money for more than ten years. Then she responded to a call to the work of Christ's Church. Seminary was personally rewarding and financially difficult. By graduation she was ready. She entered her first parish with enthusiasm, creativity, and commitment. She believed her previous experience, seminary training, and the depth of her Christian faith would make a difference in the small town church that called her as pastor.

Three years later, she wondered how she could have made such a terrible mistake. She thought ministry must not be for her. The church board had requested her resignation. She was not certain what really happened. During the first eighteen months, things seemed to be going well. There was some grumbling when she instituted changes in the order of worship and committee assignments, but she believed those changes were needed. In fact, Sue paid little attention to negative comments about the changes. In the business world she had learned that someone always complains. She understood that leadership involved doing the necessary, and she could live with the consequences.

The next eighteen months became increasingly difficult. Instead of becoming more appreciative of Sue's leadership, the people resisted more. She adhered to her banking principles. The more difficult the situation, the harder she pushed for what she believed necessary. After all, she reasoned, she was the leader of the congregation and no reasonable person could deny that each of her changes was an improvement.

By the beginning of the third year, some members of the church complained constantly. When she was new, people commended her preaching. Now they found fault with everything from content to length. People began to criticize the way she dressed, her patterns of speech, and her nervous habits. Yet Sue had great determination, and she met each challenge with new resolve.

The last month seemed more like war than a loving relationship between the shepherd and the flock. Sue was dumbfounded. "Mary and Jim have been like parents to me. They have been a constant source of counsel and support. When they came to my house and told me they were upset with my leadership I really lost it. What is wrong with this congregation? What is wrong with me? What happened?"

LESSON TO LEARN

Pastorates are not contests to see who runs the show.

Without taking into account that congregational life differs substantially from banking, Sue began to apply her business management model in her first parish. In the bank, she had authority to make decisions. She assumed she had the same authority in the church. Unfortunately, parish ministry does not normally function that way—at least not in most Protestant denominations. Congregations do not empower ministers, especially newly ordained ones, to make decisions without extensive consultation and clear consent. The laity expects more than to be informed about decisions. They want to participate in those decisions.

Sue made another mistake when she assumed she had automatic privileges or responsibilities because she was the pastor. Being seminary trained, ordained by the Church of Jesus Christ, and even called and paid by a local church means little until the congregation grants one the authority of the office of ministry.

The authority invested in those called by God to the office of ordained ministry can be traced to several sources. The most important, of course, is Scripture. The minister must demonstrate extensive knowledge of the Bible and share it with the people of the church. Additionally, tradition adds to a minister's authority. When Scripture and tradition are combined with the endorsement of the whole church, a minister has the basic ingredients of authority.

Alone these do not guarantee that a pastor will be granted the authority of ordination and installation. That happens only when the congregation becomes convinced the clergy is competent, trustworthy, committed, and caring. Consequently, the authority of the office is actualized when the congregation permits it to happen. In practice this occurs when the congregation perceives it has a quality relationship with the minister. The more the congregation trusts the pastor, the more it permits him/her to assume authority for the functions of ministry. The more pastors demonstrate their ability, the more the congregation trusts them. On the other hand, if the people do not trust the minister, do not believe he/she is committed to ministry, question his/her competence, or do not perceive they are valued by the minister, they may never invest the clergy with the authority of office.

When Sue receives her next call, she must spend more time developing a relationship before she pushes for changes. Parish ministry cannot be approached as a test of will between the minister and the congregation.

BATTLE #3

Instead of working for mutual respect, the pastor "spoils" for a fight.

For nearly twenty years Larry built a reputation as a competent pastor. It made little difference in his experience as pastor of Armageddon United Church. After four years, he left the church with serious questions not only about his pastoral abilities but also about the state of his mental health.

It started innocently enough. When he first talked with the leaders of the church about becoming their pastor, they mentioned that things had not gone well with the previous pastor. In fact, they had asked him to leave during his tenth year of service. It had something to do with the poor handling of a doctrinal dispute. Larry paid little attention to the details. He assumed the man's effectiveness was flagging after a decade of ministry.

Only later did Larry realize that there was more to it. He read the history of the church and discovered this congregation *always* fired the pastor. Other ministers in town warned him of the members of the church who were known "troublemakers." Colleagues in his own denomination shared horror stories about the reputation of the congregation. One day the former pastor of the congregation stopped to talk. Far from being the incompetent ogre the congregation described, he was a kind gentle man who shared his story of pain and disappointment with the people Larry was now trying to serve as pastor.

Within the first few months, Larry's anxiety level began to escalate. He wondered if he was to experience the same fate. He knew some congregations have an ability to "chew up" clergy. This might be one of them. He resolved never to permit a repeat of the last fellow's experience. He had no desire to become a victim of ministerial mastication.

He began to monitor his interactions with members of the congregation. Like a patient three years from cancer surgery, he overreacted to incidents. If a member of the church made a comment about the length of last week's sermon, he felt compelled to defend himself. If someone complained about the temperature in the sanctuary, he took it personally. If a committee chairperson did not follow through on an assignment, Larry suspected it an attempt to put the pastor in a bad light.

Before long, church members began to complain of harsh treatment by the pastor. When the leadership raised questions about Larry's defensiveness, he assumed they were against him as well.

Within two years, Larry was having at least one verbal confrontation per week with church members. By the fourth year, the stress on the congregation as well as Larry and his family was unbearable. The atmosphere of Sunday morning worship was electric with anger. Even casual conversations between the pastor and church members frequently erupted into disagreements.

As predicted, Larry became another pastoral casualty at Armageddon United Church. Larry resigned before the church board could terminate him. On his last Sunday morning, he lectured the congregation on their cruelty to ministers, but the congregation paid little attention. In their estimation, Larry's unprofessional behavior could be explained only by postulating mental illness.

LESSON TO LEARN

Knights who fight fire-breathing dragons often get burned.

Larry was burned by the congregation he believed to be a fire-breathing dragon. The day Larry began to consider himself as locked in mortal combat with the forces of evil, he established a pattern of acting and reacting that undermined any chance of effective ministry.

Although the extreme to which Larry carried the battle is rare, ministers frequently come to think of the congregation as the enemy and of himself/herself as either the defenseless victim or the knight in shining armor battling the forces of evil. Most congregations do not appreciate the comparison. This attitude also creates a no-win situation for the minister. When the members of the church are treated as the enemy, they tend to respond accordingly. When this happens, serious problems are inevitable. In describing the difference between the deacons and the devil, Charles Spurgeon put his finger on the problem: "Resist the devil and he will flee from you. Resist the deacons and they will fly at you." The pastor who approaches local church ministry as if it were a war to be fought will lose.

In fact, any time the relationship between the congregation and pastor resembles a battlefield rather than a relationship of mutual care and respect, the minister *and* the church lose.

A BETTER WAY TO BUILD A RELATIONSHIP

To be the pastor of a local church one must love the people of God and be committed to enabling them to grow in their faith. The person who does not love people enough to be concerned about their spiritual growth should seriously consider making a living some other way. Good intentions are not, however, enough. A minister can fail to establish a caring relationship with the people he/she seeks to love.

H. G. Wells' short story "The Pearl" tells of a bereaved man who spent a fortune building a crypt to house the remains of his beloved wife. The project took years. When finished the man concluded everything was perfect with one exception—the casket did not meet the artistic standards of its surroundings. It could not remain in the crypt.

Many of us enter ministry because we want to serve the Lord by loving his people and being a part of a caring community, yet somewhere during the journey our good intentions become sidetracked.

During the years of preparation, theological concerns may replace the importance of people. The daily routine of greasing the ecclesiastical machinery may acquire a higher priority than the people the machinery is intended to serve. One can easily lose sight of the fact that ministry involves loving people. This caring will not happen without a meaningful relationship between people and pastor.

To remain open to building such a relationship, keep these principles in mind:

Assume that members of the congregation are fellow strugglers in the Christian way.

Any other assumption undermines the relationship. The minister who arrives in the parish expecting the people to demonstrate their trust before a loving relationship is established ensures that an insulted congregation will soon draw the battle lines.

Assume people have progressed on their Christian journey.

Resist making "An Introduction to the New Testament" the first course taught in each new parish. Do not assume that people in the congregation are at the beginning of their faith journey. Every person will be at a different place in his/her spiritual life. Some will, without a doubt, be newcomers to the faith. However, the pastor must be willing to give people credit for having had experience with the gospel before he/she arrived.

Assume people are more likely Christians who are hurting and in need of a healing word rather than pagans in need of punishment.

The typical congregation has significant needs. One in five will be grieving; one in three married people will be facing problems capable of destroying that marriage; at least half the congregation, it may be assumed, have problems adjusting in school, work, home, or community which endanger their happiness. To these estimates one must add those who suffer depression, anxiety, and guilt.

Ministers are trained to help hurting people. We are not trained as warriors or asked to equate the congregation with the forces of evil. If the minister comes to the church anticipating a battle, he/she will set in motion a self-fulfilling prophecy. Rather than doing battle, we function best as instruments of God's love to a hurting people.

This must be kept in perspective. When a parishioner calls to read the riot act, it is difficult not to become irritated and to lash out. When a family with all manner of turmoil in its private life decides to use the pastor as a scapegoat, it is difficult not to take it personally. Reacting angrily, however, only complicates matters. We are called to be instruments of healing, not warriors on the ecclesiastical battlefield.

Assume pastoral ministry means loving people into wholeness, not winning battles.

Congregations in which the people do not feel loved and appreciated are troubled. We are, after all, in the business of loving people and using things. Even those who have responded to the high calling are not immune to twisting priorities until we use people and love things.

HINTS FOR RELATIONSHIP MAINTENANCE

Effective, satisfied pastors keep the fences mended with the congregation. This requires constant maintenance. The relationship between pastor and congregation can never be taken for granted. Consider these as necessary tools for the job.

1. *Accept the inevitability of conflict, criticism, and hassles.*

Such acceptance helps keep things in perspective and makes it possible to endure the tough times with a bit of good humor. The alternative, to expect the relationship to be trouble free, ensures you will be driven to insanity.

2. *Learn the wisdom of silence.*

The pastors who maintain good relationships with their congregations bite their tongues with great regularity. Say none of the following: "If you had been at the last board meeting/worship service/committee meeting as you were supposed to be, you would have known that!" "I don't care how much she appreciates my visits, I cannot visit her on a daily basis." "If you listened once in a while you might have heard me say that." "Since you know so much on the topic, why don't we have you preach a sermon series on it." "I told you so." As good as it might feel to make those comments, the pastor pays too high a price in terms of guilt, escalating conflicts, and damage to relationships.

3. *Develop ways to "be angry but sin not."*

In this Ephesian dictum, Paul challenges us to find non-destructive ways to express anger. This can be done by writing angry letters detailing one's thoughts and feelings. Putting an issue into words has a therapeutic effect. Do not mail the letter immediately. Put it in the top desk drawer and wait a week. Reread it and make necessary corrections and additions. Put it back in the desk and wait another week before reading and revising it again. In three weeks you will be grateful that the letter was not mailed. This technique provides a marvelous way to "give them a piece of your mind" without the consequent furor such an activity normally generates.

4. *Don't package your self-identity in your sermons or your program.*

As certain as the sun comes up in the East, someone will be critical of the ways things are being done at the church, particularly the way a certain topic was handled in a sermon. While frequently constructive, criticism can also be an irrational, emotional reaction to other things happening in the person's life. Sometimes criticisms are offered as nothing more than vicious comments intended to wound and not to heal. Whatever the intent, the pastor must be ready. Though not easy, learn not to take criticism personally. The minister typically invests so much of himself/herself in sermons, programs, and even ideas that they become like his/her children. However, to take inevitable criticisms personally and to respond as if they were attacks on your personhood escalates conflict unnecessarily. By putting distance between one's self-worth and one's work, the relationship between pastor and congregation stays much healthier. In turn, the pastor experiences greater satisfaction and effectiveness.

5. *There are usually several solutions to the same problem.*

As a group, ministers tend to be inflexible. We tend to believe we know the only way things should be done. On the other hand, every congregation has several members with this same tendency. Trouble comes when the solution proposed by the bull-headed minister does not agree with the one being supported by the equally stubborn layperson.

Fortunately, the problem can be mediated. God has created a world in which most problems have multiple solutions. Every difference of opinion need not escalate into a contest producing a winner. In the local church, if the pastor wins, the layperson loses. When that happens, the relationship suffers. Keeping the peace and building bridges of understanding require that one learn to listen for alternative solutions to the same problem.

6. *Remember the value of a sweet word.*

The writer of Proverbs reminds us: "Kind words are like honey—sweet to the taste and good for your health" (Prov. 16:24 GNB). The abundant use of kind and positive words strengthens both the speaker and the hearer.

Do not overlook this principle. People often mistakenly believe that every negative situation must be addressed and every positive one can be taken for granted. Rather, the liberal use of kind words and messages of appreciation are essential for building every relationship, including those in the church.

Consider implementing a Five-for-One Plan in the congregation. Under this arrangement the pastor or any member of the congregation may discuss a problem or make a complaint only after making five positive comments. This program has several direct benefits. It breaks ingrained negative patterns of thinking, provides a more accurate reflection of the actual relationship in the congregation between problems and blessings, and even becomes a game the congregation and pastor play to replace the let's-complain-about-everything-we-can-think-of game. Finally, such an intentionally positive discussion helps both congregation and pastor not to take themselves too seriously. In fact, this program usually introduces a bit of humor. Being able to laugh at ourselves and our situation helps get us through some difficult times.

CHAPTER III

BALANCE THE MINISTERIAL OFFICES

What a curious sight! The one-man band beat on a drum; clanged cymbals between his knees; moved his mouth between the harmonica, clarinet, and trumpet fastened around his neck as he played a piano with his free hand. What a skillful fellow. With his ability to make music by keeping so many things going simultaneously, he should consider the ministry.

Congregational ministry offers incredible diversity. Not many occupations provide the opportunities to have as many different experiences as the pastorate. As one of the few remaining generalists, pastors counsel the troubled, marry the romantic, bury the dead, organize the disorganized, chastise the errant, and console the grieving. Clergy meet as many people as storekeepers, attend as many committee meetings as legislators, and keep a social calendar to exhaust a celebrity. The pastor also engages in enough study, prayer, and meditation to make the profession a nice mix of the academic and the monastic. What other calling offers such variety!

More than a source of challenge and excitement, practicing this diversity brings satisfaction. As good physical health depends on a balanced diet, the pastor's positive emotional health depends on a balance among the job's many demands, expectations, opportunities, and disciplines. The more skills developed, freedoms exercised, activities engaged in, and challenges met, the more fulfilling the ministry. The fewer the activities, the fewer challenges accepted, and the more specialized the ministry, the more likely the pastor will find the high calling to pastoral ministry a bumpy road.

Learning how to enjoy the diversity of the pastorate rather than be overwhelmed by it requires considerable experimentation, expertise, and experience.

The generalized work of pastoral ministry offers both hazards and opportunities. We risk being thought incompetent and old-fashioned as we run against the trends. Nearly every other profession continues to move toward narrower specialization. Only pastors, elementary school teachers, and general practice physicians can accurately be called generalists. Of course, we can reasonably counter these charges by noting that the fragmentation caused by increased specialization makes the who-listic pastoral ministry even more essential. It also makes the local church pastor one of the most competent people for helping others deal with the range of problems that inflict society.

In an extremely helpful article on this topic, James Dowd notes that the hazards of being a generalist are intensified by the fact that pastors are taught and advised by specialists.[1] The people who teach the seminary classes seldom are the same ones who work year-in and year-out as parish ministers. Very seldom does a minister with fifteen to twenty years of solid parish experience get into print with advice for fellow ministers. Instead the experts on pastoral ministry are specialists! While highly competent, they still write and teach about wholistic ministry for generalist pastors from a specialist's perspective. Dowd remarks, "As a result, the specialists who teach and advise us about our work often talk and write as if their particular specialty, whether preaching or counseling, education or managing, deserves at least half of our time."

CLERGY MUST TEND THE DUTIES OF OFFICE

In the *Institutes of the Christian Religion,* John Calvin discusses the pastoral minister's role of prophet, priest, and king, or, in keeping with a more inclusive ministry, "wise ruler." When the minister calls the church to human love and justice by challenging, comforting, and warning, the role of prophet is practiced. Consoling, accepting, forgiving, and comforting are priestly functions. Acting as

1. James F. Dowd, "The Pastor as Generalist," *The Pastor's Newsletter,* ed. Richard Watts, vol. 4, October, 1983.

wise ruler involves the effective administration of
the resources God has given the church.

Calvin made a valid point about three mandatory
activities. The institutional health of the church
requires prophetically challenging messages from
the pulpit, loving pastoral care in times of need, and
wise governance. None can be practiced to the
exclusion of the others. The church suffers when
ordained leadership attempts to be prophetic
without being pastoral. Pastoral care provided to
the exclusion of the call for justice distorts the
gospel. Neither the prophetic nor the priestly roles
can be effectively practiced without the gentle yet
intentional guidance of an effective administrator.
The institution withers without a wise ruler.
Without adequate attention to administrative
duties, the people eventually stop coming to church.
On the other hand, ministry requires more than an
able manager. Ministers must be businesslike
without mistaking the church for a business. The
congregation pastored by an able manager who
offers neither prophetic word nor adequate pastoral care, offers a poor witness of God's love.

The health and well-being of the institution and
the pastor require a balance among the roles of
prophet, priest, and wise ruler. As an unbalanced
diet weakens physical health and makes a person
susceptible to illness, unbalanced ministries weaken
clergy and make them susceptible to pastoral
despair.

The difficulty, of course, comes in knowing when
these roles are balanced. A physician has tests to
indicate when a diet needs more protein or less fat.
From the test results, prescriptions can be written.
Empirical tests do not exist, however, to determine

if the pastor is adequately prophetic, overly priestly, or administratively malnourished. One cannot diagnose if "the spirit is depleted of compassion," or know if a prescription to cut two hours per week out of your counseling load and spend an extra hour preparing your sermon will restore joy and effectiveness.

In lieu of scientific tests, diagnoses, and prescriptions, the practicing minister must rely on reading the symptoms to indicate when the pastoral functions are out of balance. While not as accurate as a blood test or a full-body CT scan, the presence of any of the following symptoms indicates that one or more of the functions of ministry may be out of balance.

You might be overemphasizing the role of priest when—

—your weekly counseling load approaches that of a full-time psychologist.
—making a hundred and fifty home visits per month leaves no time for sermon preparation.
—upon returning from late night church meetings, you have an uncontrollable urge to phone shut-ins "just to see how they are."
—your sermons deal only with the personal problems being faced in the congregation.
—you never refer troubled people to other counselors or agencies because you perceive doing so makes you pastorally negligent.
—the people need you so much in their homes you can never be found in the office.
—committee meetings are believed primarily times

of pastoral care and only secondarily times to do the business of the church.

—the only recent books in your library are on counseling.

—you never take a vacation lest someone will need you when you are gone.

—every continuing education event in the past five years has been concerned with developing, sharpening, and expanding your skills in pastoral care.

You may need to work harder on priestly duties when—

—a key leader of the church was in the hospital for three weeks and you did not find time to visit her.

—you fall asleep during marriage counseling sessions.

—you refer every counseling opportunity.

—other than writing the sermon, little or no time is spent preparing for worship.

—you never ask "How are you?" lest you be forced to listen to the answer.

—you do not realize that even committee meetings offer convenient opportunities for pastoral care.

You may be taking the prophetic role too seriously when—

—every sermon deals with issues of justice, world peace, and other social issues.

—even your conversation during nursing home visits concerns world hunger.

—you are so concerned that the congregation be aware of the basic inequalities of the world that you constantly scold them for being so rich.

—you spend more time serving on community action committees than in sermon preparation and pastoral visitation combined.
—you refuse to perform the funeral for a church member because you did not agree with his racial attitude.
—the only recent books in your library are on social issues.
—peace conferences are the only continuing education events you attend.

On the other hand, you may be prophetically negligent when—

—you never preach on controversial issues for fear the congregation may get angry with you.
—you never permit others to preach to your congregation lest they say something to upset them.
—thoughts of possible nuclear war never come to mind.
—you are more concerned about the percent of next year's raise for the pastor than the percent of people who go to bed hungry every night or the fact that your congregation's world outreach budget has been reduced three consecutive years.
—you are more concerned about being liked by the congregation than publicly stating your beliefs on controversial issues.

You may be overly concerned with church administration when—

—every year you have to purchase another four-drawer cabinet to store personal files.
—you can always be found in the office.

—more time is spent formulating plans, completing records, and organizing information than on any other ministerial activity.
—the only recent books in your library concern the institutional health of local congregations.
—management books are your source of devotional reading.

You may need to be more intentional about church administration if—

—you have no plans for next year.
—you do not need a filing cabinet.
—you are not sure why you have an office.
—you never take time to read the mail or answer phone calls.
—you think the term "goal" applies only to hockey and soccer.

The presence of these, or any of the near endless symptoms that could be listed, indicates an unbalanced ministry. Failing to establish a proper mix among the roles of priest, prophet, and wise ruler results in less than good health for both the pastor and the congregation.

GUIDELINES FOR A BALANCED MINISTRY

The point of maximal balance among the offices of ministry moves constantly. At times the administrative load rightly requires most of the pastor's time and energy. At other times, the role of prophet must have greater emphasis than priest or wise ruler. Every day that passes could be devoted exclusively to priestly duties. The minister must constantly determine a healthy balance for both the pastor and the congregation.

The following guidelines and strategies make it easier to determine where balance can be found.[2]

1. *Decide which pastoral tasks are essential at this time in this situation.*

Although we constantly move from prophet to priest to administrator, we do not do everything connected with each role equally, at all times. The cycles of the church year and the pastorate require continuous decisions about the essentials of the present moment. When first called to a congregation, you must get acquainted. This could take from a few months to two years of high priority visitation. During this time of getting acquainted, you will do more listening to people's joys and hurts than implementing administrative goals. After having established yourself through this time of intense pastoral care, you can turn your attention to other matters. Benign neglect can be the standard after these visits are completed. Then, every few years, home visitation must be done more intensely. During these times of heavy visitation, one must lighten up on other denominational and administrative involvements.

This practice of tradeoffs has application in structuring the church year. During Lent, the time required for worship service preparation increases dramatically. Do not undertake additional community responsibility in the spring. When the church stewardship campaign demands administrative attention, limit outside commitments. Do not plan family vacations early in December. Advent pro-

---

2. The structure for these strategies comes from James Dowd's article.

grams limit the possibilities of time away from the church.

2. *Be specific about goals for church and ministry.*

Conduct an annual planning retreat with the church board. At this meeting every committee should report in writing its objectives for the year, and the minister should also report his/her objectives for the year. These reports become the benchmark for the year. They provide a standard for deciding what is expected of the minister as well as what is expected of the congregation. Subsequent board meetings become occasions for reporting progress toward accomplishing those goals.

Numerous benefits accrue from this simple procedure: (1) It provides specific and measurable criteria for evaluating church life; (2) the minister has annual input into deciding the essential tasks in his/her ministry; (3) this meeting annually raises the question in the pastor's mind, What changes need to be made in what I am doing?

Almost as important, the clear articulation of goals and expectations removes one of the hazards of ministerial performance—vagueness. For instance, many congregations want to improve the youth program but fail because they do not agree on what that means. One congregation had a series of youth ministers judged inadequate because they did not develop a good youth program.

The congregation, however, never set a clear standard for what they expected. It finally occurred to them that the problem might be unrealistic expectations more than the youth pastors. A meeting was called of parents and leaders interested in the youth program. They asked several basic questions. If they had a good youth program, what would it look like? Specifically, how can a good youth program be built? Who will be responsible for what?

They discovered that the vague hopes people had about youth ministry could not withstand the bright light of clear articulation. Most of these hopes sprang from comparisons with Downtown Megachurch and its three-hundred member touring youth choir or from distant memories of what worked when they were young. These notions were unrealistic for that congregation, at that time, in that community. When objectives for a realistic program took shape, they discovered that parents and other lay leaders could do the job as effectively as the youth pastor. In fact, they realized that many successful youth programs introduce conflict in congregations by establishing young people's church within the church of their parents. They wanted their youth program integrated with congregational life rather than apart from it.

The group developed a set of goals and objectives for the next four years. Lay leadership became central to the youth program. Within two years, youth meeting attendance went from an average of fifteen to an average of sixty-five participants. Youth Sunday now has over one hundred participants leading worship. The youth minister became the coordinator of the program, but not necessarily the sponsor.

3. *Whenever possible, allow one task to serve more than one purpose.*

The rounds of routine home visits one makes upon arrival in a community are also sources of program ideas and suggestions of direction the church might be taking. They provide an opportunity to accomplish one of the most significant pastoral tasks: learning the congregational mindset. Every community has its own way to think about and talk about the issues. Every region of the country has its own variations of language and thought. The wise pastor gets to know the uniqueness of the community early in the ministry. If one fails to do so, late in the ministry comes earlier than expected. These home visits also provide the opportunity to discover the talents and interests of the membership. This information can be beneficial in later recruitment of lay leaders.

The study one does for sermons can serve as material for a Bible study group. Sermons can frequently be reworked into talks for small church groups. Sermon illustrations can be used two years later for the minister's article in the weekly newsletter. Form letters and invocations for community meetings can always be reworked and reused.

4. *Be a specialist, but only a temporary one.*

Although we are generalists, we can concentrate on one subject or area of ministry for a few months or even a couple of years.

For example, a minister might be located in a community that does not have good marriage counselors to whom he/she can refer troubled couples. What a great opportunity to learn to do this important ministry. In the next community this skill might not be needed nearly as frequently and one can specialize in a different ministry.

The pastorate offers this opportunity to make changes in the direction and focus of one's ministry.

Doing so enhances both the satisfaction and the effectiveness.

5. *Keep essential tasks under control.*

Ministers are often tempted to concentrate too heavily on the tasks at which they are most proficient and slight those they do not enjoy. If one does not enjoy preaching, numerous other activities will keep one from sermon preparation. If one proves competent at counseling, the demands can overwhelm. Do not succumb to the temptation to do what you want to do and neglect what you do not want to do. Set minimums and maximums. If you enjoy counseling, decide the maximum number of times you will see a person about a problem. If personal problems go beyond these limits, make a referral to a professional counselor. If tempted to spend too much time in sermon preparation, set a limit on how many hours you will spend at the task. On the other hand, force yourself to set aside time to do tasks you dislike. At least once a year, do a self-evaluation and redistribute your work load to be certain that all pressing essential tasks are fairly and adequately handled.

6. *Use quality time for quality tasks.*

Ministers must accommodate their idiosyncrasies. If you know you are a morning person, rise early enough to do work that requires concentration and creativity before noon. Study and write in the morning. The afternoons can be devoted to calling and perfunctory administrative tasks. If you are an afternoon or evening person adjust your schedule accordingly. Knowing one's personal rhythm makes it possible to distribute the work load to interface tasks with abilities.

7. *Use the calendar and the clock to set limits.*

A minister must set intentional limits on the amount of time he/she will devote to ministry. There will always be more demands than can be met in all the hours of the day and the days of the week. The pastor cannot expect to complete every task. Therefore, the pastor must determine his/her own schedule by limiting time commitments rather than permitting congregational demands to determine the time spent on ministry.

Consider this strategy for placing limits on the time devoted to ministry:

(a) *The previously committed evening.* Establish certain days and evenings for personal use. Schedule these times for family or for self as you would schedule every other appointment. When asked, say, "Sorry, I already have an appointment that night."

(b) *Multiple meeting nights.* Conserve evenings by having only two or three committee nights per month. As many as four committees can meet in the same evening. The pastor can move from meeting to meeting. The committees function just as well with this limited pastoral input.

(c) *Personal development time.* Be certain to schedule time for yourself. This might be for a program of regular exercise, shopping, home chores, or just a walk in the woods. Be hard-nosed about keeping some time for yourself.

The uniqueness of each pastor, congregation, and their relationship complicates the search for proper balance among the roles of office. What functioned well with one congregation does not work well with the next. Even what worked two years ago with the same congregation may cause problems today. The mixture of roles that was once enormously satisfying may be a source of present frustration. These strategies are intended to help locate the point of maximal balance. The effective minister, however, must constantly work to maintain the right balance among the offices of ministry according to the time and the congregation. This is never a simple task.

CHAPTER IV

RISE ABOVE BUSYNESS

A Presbyterian colleague laments the time spent in meetings. "I have this recurring nightmare," he says. "My wife and five children gather at the cemetery for my funeral. At the close of the service, the funeral home director approaches my weeping family and hands them a box containing all my earthly possessions. In the box are thirty-five years of my annual calendars. I read over their shoulders as they scan the appointment notes that kept me busy for so many years. It occurs to me how seldom anything of significance was ever accomplished at those gatherings. I turn to look at my tombstone. The epitaph reads, 'Daddy has gone to another meeting.' "

Similar thoughts bubble from the psyche of many pastors. After the initial adjustment, pastoral schedules are busy. Someone always needs a visit. Another meeting needs attending. Some task always needs to be completed. The demands of congregation, community, and denomination always threaten to overwhelm the minister.

For more than thirty-five years, John pastored congregations of various sizes. Currently he serves on a middle judicatory staff. Recently he reminisced about advice given by a fellow minister. After many years in the pastorate, this man became a hospital chaplain. "Remember, John," the colleague told him, "there are many forms of ministry other than the pastorate. The local church can wear you out. Later in life you might want to think about some other form of ministry."

"I thought he just could not cut the mustard," John said. "Now I realize he was merely telling it like it is. In fact, it is a truth I frequently pass on to other ministers. Pastoral ministry is extremely demanding work. It wears you out."

Congregations seem to defy all natural laws of momentum. Local churches require constant effort to make things happen. When the pushing ceases, so does the movement. Typically, the pastor has the responsibility to keep things going and the task never ends.

Auto tires used to have synthetic cord added for strength. An acquaintance told of seeing the process by which the cord was installed. He described an enormous room of spinning spools of rayon cord.

As each spool emptied, a man tied the end of the string to a full spool. He repeated the process for literally hundreds of spools. The scene resembled the proverbial one-armed paper hanger. For eight hours each day, this frantic fellow raced about tying fresh spools of cord onto the last bits of string from emptying spools. As the assembly line did not stop, the man could not stop. He was always alert, always on the run. If he failed to do his job, the manufacturing process ground to a halt.

The pastoral ministry requires constant activity accompanied by the unrelenting responsibility to keep it going. For this reason, many ministers find the county fair a remedial necessity for the busyness of parish life. One full week each year the pastor can wander the midway aimlessly, talk with friends, watch the frantic activity, and take delight in thinking, "All this happens and I don't have to do a thing to keep it going."

HEALTHY REASONS TO BE BUSY

Since there are both benefits and hazards in the busyness of the pastorate, begin by examining a few positive reasons to be busy.

Busyness is being one of the last generalists in an age of specialists.

As mentioned in the previous chapter, we live in a time of specialization. The complexity of the age limits the functioning of generalists. Yet the ministry persists as a generalist profession.

Serving the local church does not permit one to specialize in one activity to the exclusion of all others. Few congregations are of sufficient size to permit the pastor to preach but not call on the sick, to counsel without accepting administrative responsibility, or to be involved in the community without performing weddings and funerals. Obviously this diversity of responsibility keeps the pastor busy.

It has been argued that the generalist nature of the pastorate diminishes its prestige. This argument reflects a secular mind-set. In most other fields, the narrower the specialty, the greater the honor and the better the pay. For this reason, many clergy hunger and thirst after the specialized ministries. Seminary teachers, pastoral counselors, and hospital or institutional chaplains are often thought of as holding more respectable jobs than the poor pastor slogging along in the local church.

Actually, specialized vocations should not be envied. Multitudes spend years training for specialized work only to be bored by insufficient diversity. By the time people realize they do not like what they are doing they are trapped by education and income. Highly specialized skills cannot easily be transferred to other fields and high salaries are not easily replaced.

Pastoral ministry, on the other hand, offers the satisfaction of diverse activity. The "people skills" of ministry are more easily transferred to other fields, and pastoral salaries are more readily matched and exceeded.

Because the local church requires the services of a generalist rather than a specialist, the pastor will be busy. The busyness of diversity, however, is a source of significant joy.

Busyness can result from the broad definitions of ministry.

Pastoral ministry has no easily defined boundary. Lawyers know when they are practicing law and when they are doing something else. The same can be said for selling insurance, building cars, or working at nearly every other job. This is not true for ministry, a profession without natural borders.

Many clergy stop regularly at the same place for coffee, doughnuts, conversation, and the opportunity to read a free newspaper supplied by the management. If we were employed in industry, we would say we stopped on the way to work. As ministers, we can make a good case that our workday starts at the restaurant. We know all the regulars. We have counseled with them, visited them in the hospital, attended their family funerals, and even received a few into membership of the church. Our stops at the doughnut shop are part of the job. After all, we do the same things there we do during the remainder of the day.

Ministers never actually get away from it all. We can be called on for the duties of ministry at any time of the day or night. As the business of enabling and caring for the people of God, ministry can become so broadly defined it can include almost anything. A member of our local United Way board commented on the problem they have allocating charitable dollars to worthwhile agencies. "The Christian Home Mission just won't stay out of other people's areas," he said. "They want to feed people, provide housing and give counseling. We already fund agencies to do those things. We cannot pay for two groups to do exactly the same thing. I fear I will call down there some day and be told I cannot talk to Pastor Johnson, the director, because he is in the operating room doing surgery on some needy fellow who came in off the street."

Because it does not have easily defined boundaries, the pastor can always be involved with ministry. Rather than a problem, this is a source of joy. After all how many people can claim a trip to the coffee shop as part of the day's work?

Busyness grows from relationships.

The longer an effective minister serves the same parish, the more relationships he/she will develop with people and the busier he/she will be. An older priest of the Order of Friar Minor claimed, "I ask to be transferred every two years. It is the only way I have time for myself. If I do not move with regularity, this one wants me to do something for that one and that one wants me to do something for someone else. There is no end to it. I love people, but the demands drive me nuts."

Although we might disagree with his method of handling it, he put his finger on an issue in pastoral ministry. Ministry as a "people business" requires extensive relationships. The longer one stays in a parish, the deeper the relationships become. Busyness grows from these relationships. It cannot be avoided and, in fact, should not be avoided.

NOT SO HEALTHY REASONS FOR BUSYNESS

The busyness arising from being a generalist who develops growing relationships with people in the context of a vocation without boundaries can be a source of problems as well as joys.

The problem is being a generalist.

Frustration can result from a generalist vocation. To be a generalist often means not having enough training, experience, and/or time to see things to completion. It means making referrals and never hearing how things turned out, having more irons in the fire than can be reasonably handled and often having to live with the feeling of being condemned to doing things haphazardly rather than well.

Growing relationships can become burdensome.

The maintenance of any relationship requires emotional and spiritual energy. As counseling sessions, hospital calling, and funeral home visits obviously require such energy, so does the maintenance of relationships with committees, ministerial colleagues, and personal friends. Complicating matters even further, the longer one remains in a parish, the deeper and more numerous the relationships. No wonder ministers have little strength left to develop family relationships.

The warmth, friendliness, and outgoing personality helpful in the pastorate can also be liabilities. The person who does a good job developing relationships increases the number and depth of those relationships. The more relationships, the more energy expended and the more likely one will burn out.

Effective ministers come to understand that they must put limits on their relationships. Occasionally they find it necessary to resign from a service club or to refuse to meet one more family who live in the neighborhood but do not belong to the church. The longer they are in a community, the more restrictive they must become on the weddings they perform for couples outside the congregation. Rather than withdrawal from the human community, they have come to accept that when primary relationships deepen, they must economize in beginning secondary new ones.

Where there are no boundaries, there is no strength.

The lack of boundaries to the ministry threatens the health and well-being of the pastor by pulling him/her in too many directions simultaneously. The Bear River in northern Michigan starts at Walloon Lake and empties into Lake Michigan. While the actual distance is only twenty miles, the river bed winds and turns lazily for more than a hundred miles like some giant serpent sunning itself. The banks of the shallow stream are wide and the water flows with little power. As it approaches Lake Michigan, the banks narrow to a spillway about one-tenth as wide. The results are dramatic. Instead of wandering, the river flows straight and the once lazy stream becomes torrential.

When the pastor wanders from task to task without a sense of direction, he/she loses strength like the wide, meandering river. The flexibility of the broadly based definition of ministry can be an asset. It can also be a liability. To avoid losing direction and power, experienced and satisfied ministers continually evaluate, reassess, and prioritize pastoral work.

Ministers are frequently compulsive people in a compassionate profession.

Generally speaking, people who enter ministry need to be needed. We appreciate the feedback we get from serving the needs of others. A minister cannot, however, meet every person's every need. Someone always has a hurt to be mended or a tear to be dried. Unlike building a bridge, the job of helping people has no logical stopping place. When one adds this aspect to the compulsive nature of many ministers, becoming overwhelmed by busyness approaches the inevitable.

SOME PAINFUL PASTORAL REALITIES

There can be too much of a good thing. The same characteristics that are satisfying can become frustrating. On the other hand, some dangers of busyness can be traced to other aspects of ministry.

Ministers can be burned by splattering venom.

Ministry mediates the power, love, and mercy of God through preaching and pastoral care. When performing this function with healthy, positive people, effectiveness and satisfaction come easily. However, ministers must also deal with hurting people, negative people, and the emotionally and/or physically sick.

Some of the sick are filled with hatred, anger, disappointment, greed, and other assorted "poisons" of the human spirit. One of the healing ministry's least pleasant and most dangerous aspects is helping drain the venom from these sick souls. Like working with any toxic chemical, one can be severely injured.

Hurting people frequently feel free to let it all hang out within the life of the church in general and toward the pastor specifically. The security of grace permits people to express themselves willingly and often irrationally. After all, civility has never been a precondition for God's love.

Whatever the theology, those living under difficult circumstances frequently take out their frustrations on the church and her representative, the pastor. When one cannot reasonably yell at the boss about his inflexibility, at the kids for their irresponsibility, at the spouse for being sick, at parents for aging, or at God for the inherent unfairness of life itself, the pastor makes a convenient target. The regularity with which this happens suggests that multitudes believe part of the pastoral job description is to be "dumped on."

While it is never easy for pastors, the experienced ones learn not to take it personally. On the other hand, draining the venom from sick souls while avoiding being splattered by the venom consumes an enormous amount of energy. If a pastor spends too much time doing it or fails to take every emotional, professional, and spiritual precaution, he/she can be severely hurt, if not destroyed, by this difficult aspect of ministry.

Ministers can be frustrated by attempts to satisfy the insatiable.

Ministers, by nature, want to help others. This is, after all, part of the calling to servanthood. Ministers must also be concerned about doing right in the eyes of God. The rub comes in trying to discern the right in the midst of numerous, conflicting, and persistent claims.

To more fully understand the problem, save one month's mail asking the pastor to send money, attend a meeting, or rally the saints to support a cause. The typical pastor receives a staggering amount of this sort of communication. Dozens of organizations regularly ask ministers to become involved with everything from pro-life to pro-choice, resettling to giving sanctuary to refugees, supporting free speech to stamping out pornography, supporting gay rights to doing away with all homosexual rights.

Additionally, the middle judicatory and denomination will send numerous communications on promoting participation in a myriad of activities beyond the local church as well as promoting the financial support of those activities. Just thinking about the administration, promotion, and funding of these activities can be overwhelming. The sheer number of important issues boggles the mind. The local pastor can be certain, however, some organization, friend, or stranger will be in touch to urge him/her to take a stand on each and every one of them. Utter weariness can result from attempting to support every worthy idea, cause, and program.

Those who do the urging are seldom fully appreciative. Advocates usually devote their entire lives to a single issue. Sympathy with them never suffices. You must be as committed as they are. Frankly, one cannot be as committed to one hundred causes as the single-issue person is to his/hers. Pastors, caught by the self-imposed expectation to please, may attempt it, but "bedraggled schizophrenia" rather than satisfaction will result.

In a sense, the pastor serves as the frontline marketing/sales person for the Church of Jesus Christ. Consequently, we get pushed by every agency, denominational executive, and organization to market the causes and products of faith. Industry controls what managers can ask of the sales force. In the church, the Chief Operating Executive does not establish a reasonable quota for what a pastor can do. The pastor himself/herself must do that. We must choose, mediate, and filter what we are going to support and pursue. The local church pastor who does not do this can be overwhelmed by frenetic busyness.

TAKING A CLOSER LOOK AT COMPULSIVENESS

"I am convinced," a minister said in the midst of a conversation about compulsiveness, "that ministers believe they are under a different dispensation than their parishioners. We preach the laity are saved by grace, but we personally practice salvation by works. We really believe we are justified by our busyness."

Indeed, he may be right. At least a widespread myth exists among clergy that we have personal responsibility for the sun rising in the morning and the earth turning on its axis. Even when we know that neither God nor the congregation makes such a requirement, we frequently demand it of ourselves. What a pity that our self-identity should be rooted in such foolishness. We are not valued because we meet the demands of ourselves or others. We cannot measure our worth by the number of positive comments given by those who appreciate what we have done. We are loved simply because we are the children of God. We are worthwhile because God loves us, not because we have busied ourselves to the limits of human endurance doing something even as valuable as the work of Christ's church.

Postulating misplaced identity as a source of pastoral compulsiveness accounts for the anger in many pastors. Rational persons experience anger when they permit their sense of self to depend on striving for the approval of others. Sadly, some ministers are capable of generating considerable anger at leaders for not doing a good job of leading, followers for not following, those who do follow for doing so without sufficient enthusiasm, the family for making them feel guilty about not spending enough time at home, and themselves for buying into all this busyness nonsense.

A number of adjustments help us rise above busyness. For one thing, all ministers should regularly preach themselves a sermon on "Salvation by Grace." It helps keep things in perspective.

Periodically, review your personal statement on the theology of the church and ministry. God calls us to the office of ministry, not to run an office. Ministry means being an instrument of God's healing. This requires some "greasing" of the ecclesiastical machinery. It does not mean that ministers spend all their time tinkering with the machinery.

When you have a firm notion of the theology of church and ministry in mind, ask the question, "Is this the essential work of ministry or am I involved in too many nonessentials?" If the answer disturbs you, make the necessary changes.

FOLLOW THE EXAMPLE OF JESUS

The Master faced the busyness issue. The crowds pressed in and made constant demands. He could not get away from them. They even raced around the Sea of Galilee to meet his boat on the other shore. Any minister who has tried to stay in the parsonage while on vacation knows of the unrelenting demands people can make.

When the needs of the people approached the overwhelming, Jesus went away to a place of quiet for meditation and the opportunity to recenter and refocus. If Jesus knew the world could go on without him, who are we to conclude things cannot go on without us?

Jesus faced the temptations of ministry that we face. In the wilderness he had the opportunity to make his ministry totally relevant to the physical needs of people: "Command these stones to become loaves of bread." He had the chance to have a spectacular ministry: "If you are the Son of God, throw yourself down" from the pinnacle of the temple. Jesus was also tempted by political power: "All these [kingdoms] I will give you, if you will fall down and worship me." He did not succumb to any of these temptations. Instead, he kept his ministry, and thus ours, in perspective: "You shall worship the Lord your God and him only shall you serve."

In various forms, we are tempted by the lure of power, the appeal to be spectacular, and the reasonableness of being relevant. But whenever we succumb to those temptations, we are overwhelmed by the unrealistic demands they make on us. Only by the strength of the grace of God do we ever face down these temptations and properly distinguish between important business and mere busyness.

CHAPTER V

BEWARE OF "EXPLOSIVE" PEOPLE AND SITUATIONS

Marie and Darryl stumbled accidentally into an explosive situation. Darryl ably served a succession of small congregations for over twenty-five years. Marie usually was active in leadership roles, but always as the minister's wife. They served their present parish for nearly a decade, and when the children were on their own, Marie decided to work toward her lifelong goal of ordination. Her husband gave his enthusiastic support, so they began the search process. They easily found a congregation within driving distance of a seminary where they planned to work as a clergy team on weekends while Marie attended school and Darryl handled pastoral duties during the week.

When they were interviewed by the pulpit committee, they discussed their intentions fully. The committee expressed some reluctance, but Darryl and Marie believed the issue was settled. The signed contract vaguely referred to their team ministry. They had no reason to doubt that the pulpit committee had discussed the matter with the congregation.

Eight months after their arrival, Darryl and Marie resigned. The congregation was told of a "clergy team," but many did not understand the significance of the term. Some said they always thought of the minister's wife as part of the "team," but they did not understand why she should preach on Sunday morning or conduct funerals. When they thought about the minister of the church, they thought of *him*, not *her*.

Almost from the first day, Darryl and Marie had to defend themselves and their plans. It was to no avail. In less than one year, they knew they could not continue, so they resigned as a clergy team. The congregation accepted Darryl's resignation. They did not believe Marie had an office from which to resign.

Darryl and Marie had wandered unaware into a congregational mine field. Naïvely, they stepped on the most explosive issue in the church. In retrospect, Darryl and Marie realized they failed to examine the makeup of the congregation before accepting the call. There were no women in positions of leadership. Women enforced this unwritten rule, rather than the men. When Marie preached on "God's Love for All *Her* Children," she mistakenly believed the women of the church would be sympathetic to the issue she wanted to raise.

It can be argued that Darryl and Marie are models of foolishness or carelessness. However, many ministers begin ministries without knowledge of where the mines are buried. Only too late they discover that they have inadvertently detonated one. But land mine dangers should not be taken lightly. Every parish has a few. The effective pastor keeps track of where they are and treads lightly when near them. Joy in ministry requires an accurate map of parish land mines.

Effective ministry depends on developing skills for identifying and handling problem people and situations. Clergy who do not develop this ability usually have short, painful pastorates.

In the next two chapters, two very different types of people-related difficulties will be discussed. Chapter 6 deals with a type of problem which, for the most part, must be endured rather than resolved. These are the little, inevitable, nagging issues that can be compared to "piranha bites." In small numbers, they cause discomfort, but are not fatal. The danger comes with accumulation. These little hurts can block joy by chewing a ministry and the minister into little pieces.

This chapter discusses another category of people-related ministerial problems. They can be called "parish land mines," and they differ considerably from the problems discussed in the next chapter. Parish "piranha" are unavoidable, nagging and accumulative but capable of significant harm only when precautions are not taken to minimize them. "Land mines," on the other hand, are explosive problems. More than minor obstacles, these problems maim the ministry if not the career of the minister. Every minister must endure "piranha bites," but "land mines" can be avoided, defused, or exploded under controlled circumstances.

NATURAL ENVIRONMENTS FOR LAND MINES

At fourteen I traveled from my home in the Midwest to the mountains and desert of Philmont Scout Ranch. Boy Scout training included an orientation to environmental differences between New Mexico and Ohio. For us city boys, one of the most frightening differences was rattlesnakes. We did not have them in Akron. As our leaders explained, however, only disturbed rattlesnakes bite people. Therefore, stay clear of the scrub brush in the desert. If a rattlesnake was in the area, it would be under one of those bushes in the shade, trying to stay cool. For two weeks at Philmont Scout Ranch, I cut a wide swath around every low bush. I was no fool. I knew a rattlesnake could be under any one of them.

Like rattlesnakes, explosive people and situations within the local parish have natural environments. These places should be carefully marked, scrupulously avoided, or if one must be near them, approached with extreme caution.

Some people are wired for an explosion.

Some people are just plain cantankerous. For reasons known only to the Divine, every congregation has a few people with volatile personalities and explosive tendencies. The pastor must know which members are "wired with dynamite," try to control the circumstances under which they detonate, and attempt to keep self and others as protected as possible.

A colleague told of a church member with serious and unpredictable mood swings. This woman's husband claimed he never entered the house without throwing his hat in first. If it came flying back out, he put it back on his head and went to a local restaurant for dinner. When offering pastoral care to this type of member, either practice the hat throwing trick or wear bomb squad equipment.

Every congregation has equivalent personalities. Learn to identify them. Without such information the unsuspecting minister might mishandle the situation and compound the problem.

A friend was called to a congregation the week after a racial disturbance in the city. Seeing no alternative, he addressed the issue in his first sermon. He preached on the need for calm, understanding, forgiveness, openness, and compassion among the races in the city.

That afternoon the phone rang. The caller informed the pastor, "I will never set foot in that church as long as you are the minister. You have sided with those lawless Blacks, and I will not stand for it."

The minister had no information other than the fact the caller was a church member. Did he reflect the majority view? Was he a key leader in the church? Was the new minister in as much trouble as he feared?

In an attempt to get some perspective, the minister phoned the president of the congregation who told him the caller was not a regularly attending member. The caller spoke with so little credibility even his wife paid little attention to him. Having mapped and assessed the potential danger of this particular land mine, the new minister got on with the business of getting acquainted with the church.

Take advantage of the fact that church members can help identify those "wired with dynamite." After all, the congregational leaders have dealt with these people for years. They know them, and, in most circumstances, love them in spite of the way they are as well as for what they might become. As one sainted member said of a difficult person, "I think having her as a member of our Sunday school class makes all of us better Christians."

Every congregation has a pet peeve.

In addition to people with explosive potential, every congregation has certain subjects that, when approached, pose hazards to pastoral happiness and effectiveness. Each minister must be able to identify these special problems.

Bob first became aware of this phenomenon when he was a student minister. A key leader of the congregation pulled him aside before the church board meeting and said, "Bob, about seventy-five years ago someone gave this church five acres of land. We were supposed to build a parsonage on it but never did. Instead the farmers in the church plant and harvest it. The money from the crop goes toward the church budget.

"It isn't as simple as it seems," he continued. "That five acres is always the last planted in the spring and the last harvested in the fall. It is usually the worst looking field in the county. We just don't keep it up very well. To make matters worse, every spring and

every fall we have a fight about whose turn it is to
take care of it. Having that argument is almost
traditional with us. Since it is our problem, I suggest
that, when the topic comes up, you don't say
anything. Your comments would probably not be
helpful. In fact, since the preacher does not have the
farming equipment to take a turn, most of these
fellows don't really care what you think on this
particular topic. For your own good, I recommend
silence."

Through the years, Bob has praised God for this
elder and his advice. Those five acres constituted
the pet peeve of this particular congregation. Every
congregation has some equivalent. It might be the
parking lot, the annual All Church Bazaar, the
permanent funds, or decisions made by the
denominational offices.

Of course, one cannot always avoid the congregation's pet peeve. Sometimes the issue has to be
faced. When that is necessary, use the same care
given to defusing a bomb.

Some traditions are more sacred than scripture.

A United Methodist clergyman from Georgia
related his claim of having served the shortest
pastorate in the history of the conference. "It was
my first assignment as a seminary graduate. I
arrived in town on a Thursday and went immediately to the church. It was an ancient building in a tiny
town in rural southern Georgia. I could not believe
what I found. The building only had two doors and
one was unusable. A large, ugly tree completely
blocked the side entrance to the building.

"I could not imagine why the congregation
permitted the tree to stand. It was obviously a fire
hazard. The church had no emergency exit. I

decided there was no need to wait. I went back to the parsonage, unpacked my chain saw, cut down the tree, cleaned up the mess, painted the door, and waited for thanks from the congregation when they realized how decisive and hard working their new pastor was.

"It did not work out as well as I had imagined," he continued. "It seems that particular tree had quite a reputation in that part of the state. It was known as 'The Wesley Tree' because John Wesley had planted it when he visited the town long ago. The congregation was not the least pleased with me. In fact, it was less than a week later the district superintendent thought it might be a good idea to transfer me to another congregation."

The story may or may not be true. It does, however, provide a delightful illustration on how congregational traditions can become more sacred than the Scripture. Failure to identify those traditions invites an explosion.

At the first worship committee meeting the new pastor attended, a letter from the city fire inspector was read. It proclaimed that individual lighted candles in worship services were a fire hazard and recommended no open flames for Christmas Eve services.

It seemed reasonable to the committee to follow the dictates of the fire department. They decided to dispense with lighted candles at the Christmas Eve service. The new minister and the equally new committee chairperson did not know this letter came every year. The congregation's tradition of ignoring the fire inspector's letter was almost as old as lighting candles on Christmas Eve. Their decision was as popular as cutting down the Wesley Tree.

Citing the non-biblical wisdom literature that links discretion and valor, the worship committee and the new minister decided to have a candlelight service on Christmas Eve. Given the possibility of a mob lynching, it made considerable sense to ask for more fire extinguishers and to explain safety rules for burning candles rather than to ban them.

Do not attempt to cook on a bonfire. Wait for the glowing coals.

A wise seminary professor taught his students, "When the phone rings at 2:00 A.M. on a Saturday night and a voice at the other end of the line says 'Come quick, my husband has a gun. He is drunk. He is threatening to kill me,' don't go alone! Tell her, 'I will call the police and arrive soon after they come.' "

Police are trained to break up domestic fights. Ministers can be seriously injured in situations for which they have neither expertise nor equipment. The minister does his/her best work when things have calmed down and people are able to be reasonable. When people are yelling at one another, the reassuring words of the pastor cannot be heard. To state it differently, satisfaction comes to those who wait until the flames have burned to glowing coals.

This applies to all domestic quarrels and nearly all ecclesiastical battles. Periodic spontaneous explosions in the choir, the women's group, the men's group and between certain church members are a normal part of congregational life. Unless specifically asked, one should control the urge to plunge in as mediator. Even then, great caution should be practiced. We clergy often have delusions of grandeur when it comes to evaluating our abilities as reconcilers. We also have significant difficulty distinguishing when we are actually needed from when we need to be needed.

When we control our urge to rescue long enough to permit the conflict to quiet down, we can usually put our skills to work more effectively. To leap unnecessarily into the heat of battle only guarantees getting burned.

Every congregation has people with whom the pastor will disagree.

Never expect an entire congregation to agree with the minister on all matters. Some members will always hold radically different opinions on social issues, politics, and theology. Some members of the church will hold views the pastor finds appalling. Other members will be racists. The pastor will frequently have good reason to believe the religious views of other members fall far short of orthodox Christianity. Still other members will have political opinions that do not deserve recognition within the Christian understanding of human community.

Effectiveness depends on learning to live with and work with different and disagreeable people. This frequently pushes one's patience to the outer limits. Seldom, however, is it productive to openly confront and argue with these people. Being scolded by the pastor does not change them. In fact, the pastor frequently appears inflexible and foolish. Instead learn to offer an NSN—"noncommittal smiles and nods." Instead of arguing, the wisest immediate response may be a pleasant smile and a fervent prayer not to push through one's lips the full force of what is on one's mind. Intercessory prayer and preaching introduce lasting positive change possibilities more effectively than angry confrontation.

The multiple-staff church is a special type of land mine.

The pastoral ministry can be rather lonely. Sharing the ministry of a congregation on a multiple staff can relieve the loneliness. What a pleasure to have a person who can lend a helping hand and lighten the load of the daily routine. Additionally, the multiple-staff church offers a pastor an opportunity to minister with a colleague. What a difference it makes to have a friend in an office down the hall. More than someone with whom the minister can discuss the problems, a colleague is also someone with whom to share the happy moments, to work in a trusting relationship, and with whom to be vulnerable. A ministerial staff with a healthy working relationship can be a great source of personal and spiritual growth.

On the other hand, multiple-staff ministry also has land mine potential. Most ministers are not trained to work as a team. Multiple-staff situations require a willingness to share the limelight—this is never easy. Team ministry cannot permit petty jealousy and one-upmanship. Healthy working relationships require mature, self-confident clergy.

FOUR INDISPENSABLE TOOLS FOR DEALING WITH CONGREGATIONAL LAND MINES

1. Play your trump cards carefully.

Trump cards are one of the fringe benefits of the office of ministry. These limited permissions and authority are given to the pastor by the congregation simply because he/she has been called to serve this particular fellowship. Trump cards permit the minister to get out of a personal conflict, to be forgiven an error in judgment, or to "win" a disagreement. By playing a trump card, the pastor may minimize or even avoid injury when a parish land mine explodes. As clergy begin a new relationship, the congregation gives him/her a certain number of permissible times to have his/her own way. When one decides to take advantage of one of these opportunities, a trump card is played.

When the new pastor detonated a land mine over candles on Christmas Eve, he pleaded ignorance of the tradition and the congregation forgave him. His ministry went on from there. He had to play a trump card, however, to get past the incident.

Another minister was able to get a building program passed by relying on personal esteem. "If you don't vote for this, I will resign as minister," he told them. The congregation so loved him, they voted through the building plans. To win the vote, he also had to play several trump cards.

Congregations give a varied and undisclosed number of trump cards to the pastor. Therefore they must be played carefully. Some congregations are generous, others quite stingy. What a terrible feeling to reach for a trump card during a difficult situation and discover they have all been played—some in situations far less important than the present one.

2. Know the people well.

The pastor who knows the parish and loves the people is least likely to be hurt by explosive individuals and situations. If Darryl and Marie had spent more time getting acquainted before they tried to practice a team ministry, they would have saved themselves and the congregation a great deal of pain. If they had developed a loving, working relationship with the people before Marie began to function as a minister, the team concept might have even worked. Instead, they attempted to minister before they knew the people. They did not know where the parish land mines were located. They quickly played all their trump cards and failed to build the healthy relationship that would have generated more of them. This resulted in a parish explosion that destroyed a ministry, injured a pastoral team, and hurt a congregation.

Pastoral ministry is more than a science for managing a volunteer organization. It requires the practiced art of working with and loving God's people. The key to doing this involves making people feel that they are special and that they belong to something worthwhile. A minister who relies on scolding and guilt does not value people. The minister who emphasizes the negatives to the exclusion of positives does not help people believe they are part of something important. Any approach to ministry that hurts people rather than heals, plants land mines rather than defuses them.

3. Maintain your sense of humor.

Laughter, as a gift of God, is the divine lubricant for squeaky human relationships. With a bit of laughter we not only survive the tough situations, but we can do it joyously.

It is not easy to keep a sense of humor while stepping carefully through a mine field, but it can be done. In fact, it must be done. If we take ourselves too seriously, we make situations seem worse than they are. Always keep an eye out for the humorous in the most difficult situations, the ridiculous in the midst of the serious, the ironic in the midst of the tragic.

4. In all things give thanks.

Almost anyone can be thankful when things are going well. It takes a person of great faith to be thankful for land mines. It can and must, however, be done. The call to ministry requires it.

CHAPTER VI

MINIMIZE INEVITABLE PAIN

The area ministers engaged in the usual mutual commiseration at their monthly meeting. As they went around the table each contributed to the growing tale of work, worry, meetings, crises, criticisms, problems, and weariness. Mary summarized for the group. "I knew the public nature of ministry made for a fish-bowl existence. I did not realize so many of the fish were piranha! I believe I am being eaten alive."

While quite apt, this National Geographic image needs clarification. Piranha are a genus of carnivorous fish which inhabit South American rivers and have been known to inflict wounds and even kill large animals, including humans. Contrary to popular opinion, piranha are not rare, cruel, and always deadly. They are common to most streams and they feed on passing animals because they are hungry, not because they are bent on senseless destruction. The vast majority of animals and people bitten by piranha do not die but merely contribute a bit of flesh. Very few victims are reduced to white bones floating down the river.

Travelers in that part of the world must take proper safety precautions to minimize damage done by piranhas. The fish are abundant enough that the traveler accepts the likelihood of losing an occasional bit of flesh. Seldom, however, do piranhas cause death. More typically, the person disturbs the fish and a few begin to bite. When the traveler realizes what is happening, he hurries to the other side. Only the luckiest traveler never encounters a piranha. Only the most careless die.

Crossing a South American river can be dangerous. There are also dangers inherent to pastoral ministry. Many people and situations have the potential to take a bite of flesh. Inevitably, some damage can be expected. Therefore, the pastor who desires a safe, satisfying, effective ministry must take precautions.

This does not mean that congregations are evil or that pastoral ministry is more dangerous than other occupations. It merely means that even Christian people, like piranhas, do what comes naturally. When disturbed, they bite. Therefore, a minister must keep the congregation well fed and not disturb them unnecessarily. Also remember the probability of receiving an occasional bite. Instead of expecting ministry to be easy, take precautions to minimize inevitable pain and problems, and do not make foolish sacrifices.

Generally speaking, these precautions are only common sense. Sadly, few things are more rare than common sense. Consequently, one must be explicit about some of the safety rules.

EQUIPMENT FOR MINIMIZING THE DAMAGE

Three things are mandatory for minimizing the pain of the ministry: (1) assume there will be problems and pain, (2) accept the inevitability of change, and (3) practice goal setting and planning. Assuming, accepting, and practicing these principles maximize efficiency and satisfaction by minimizing dangers.

As with life in general, ministry involves a little pain.
Unrealistically high expectations lead to misery. Multitudes fail to understand this obvious fact. Too many people are seduced by the Madison Avenue mythology about detergents for every spot and pills for every pain. Reality requires learning to live with a little discomfort. The person who refuses to accept this truth frantically attempts to solve every problem and avoid every bruise. This only intensifies pain and compounds problems. On the other hand, accepting discomfort as inevitable keeps things in perspective.

Perfection eludes every pastor and pastorate. There will be conflicts, criticisms, unfair comments, disappointing crowds, and weeks when the Sunday sermon does not fall together. To assume anything else inflicts unnecessary frustration. Accepting that ministry involves living with a certain amount of inevitable discomfort keeps things in proper perspective.

Change is inevitable.

An ancient philosopher said it well: "You never step twice into the same river." By the time the other foot gets into the water, the river moves on. Failing to realize this adds significantly to normal discomfort. For good or ill, next year things will be different. Time moves as a juggernaut. Nothing stops it, slows it down, or speeds it up. Events keep their own pace. Accept this and plan to accommodate it.

The relationship between pastor and congregation undergoes constant change. The cycle of most ministerial relationships begins with a "honeymoon." This euphoria eventually gives way to less romantic descriptions. Many clergy report having a time of rest and relaxation that some call the "Third Year Doldrums." Eventually, most clergy enter a time when it seems a good idea to seek other opportunities for ministry. This may happen during the seven-year-itch part of the cycle. Sometimes it occurs because the from-Hosanna-to-crucify-him cycle has entered its final stage.

In addition to the natural cycle in relationship to the congregation, each minister has an internal rhythm. Sometimes we are up. Sometimes we are down. Everyone's emotions are subject to change. When the down side of the minister's natural rhythm coincides with the down side of the rhythm in the relationship with the congregation, trouble erupts. The minister may misinterpret the situation: "My ministry here is over. There is nothing more I can do in this congregation. It is time to make a move." Although this could be true, the wisest pastor waits a few months to see if the natural rhythm brings another change.

Constant change invites the application of inappropriate solutions. Sam was at the church only three years when several people came with a list of minor complaints. Sam, in the doldrums anyway, took the comments personally and concluded that his effectiveness with the congregation was at an end. In a matter of weeks he secured a call to another congregation. This was the fourth time he relocated before completing four years with a church.

Sam's belief about the limit of his effectiveness may be a part of the natural cycle of congregational life. What he perceives as severe criticism may not be at all. It may take three years for people to feel comfortable enough with his leadership to bring their concerns to him. He does not know what happens after the fourth year in a relationship because he never gets there. They may be the best years. Until he stays through the down side of the normal cycle, he will never know.

Sam's system of moving when he experiences discomfort within the normal cycle of change illustrates the application of an inappropriate solution. He is like the fellow who puts an ice bag on a nosebleed when his real problem is high blood pressure. The ice temporarily stops the symptom without solving the problem. Similarly, Sam's moving temporarily stops the symptom of his dis-ease with the congregation without curing it. His third-year discomfort may only be part of his natural cycle in relationships. It may have nothing to do with severe dysfunction. Moving does not cure the problem but postpones it. If Sam endured the discomfort of the present, eventually things might improve.

It is essential to make and implement plans.

Inevitable change mandates planning. In turn, planning gives a degree of control over the direction the change takes. Having a set of goals and a plan for attaining them helps avoid the frustration of not knowing where to go and how to get there. A helpful pastoral motto is "Plan your work and work your plan."

Planning also provides a means of self-evaluation. The person who has direction, sets goals for moving in that direction, and strives to accomplish those goals, can always answer the question, What did I do this year?

Additionally, be aware of this unpublished corollary of Murphy's Law: "All unplanned change tends toward the negative." Wandering through pastoral ministry, waiting to see what will happen, usually means something bad will occur. Congregational growth, for instance, depends on implementing a plan of action. Waiting to see what might happen almost insures a decline in numbers. Goals for congregational involvement in community action or in-depth Bible study must be accompanied by plans for making them happen and plenty of hard work to implement the plans. Good intentions combined with "wait and see" efforts hardly ever result in positive change.

MISCELLANEOUS SAFETY TIPS

Accepting the necessity of living with a certain amount of pain, preparing for the inevitability of change, and maintaining an updated plan of action are important factors in minimizing ministerial mastication and maximizing pastoral effectiveness. In and of themselves they are not, of course, enough. They are only part of the total program of tools, techniques, and helpful hints every minister learns from reading, training, and pastoral experience. Although difficult, it is possible to learn from the experiences of others. It helps avoid pain and frustration. With this in mind, here are a few helpful principles for living in the piranha bowl of pastoral ministry.

It is not necessary to have a word on everything.

For many years, Lyle was one of the congregation's most active lay leaders. Although he could be relied on for any task, his special contribution was as a visitor. He was among the first callers in the homes of community newcomers. His broad smile and friendly way brought more people into membership than any other evangelistic program. When the minister was on vacation, Lyle became the congregation's hospital visitor. The warmth of his manner and the depth of his faith gave people comfort during sickness.

One day his wife called the church to say that Lyle was in the hospital for tests. His energy level was low and he had recently felt nauseated. "Nothing to worry about," she cheerfully asserted.

When his newly ordained pastor dropped by the hospital he expected the conversation to be the

usual chatter about the church and the current
World Series. Instead, Lyle informed him he had an
acute form of cancer and was not expected to live
more than six months.

The young pastor was unprepared for the news.
This was the first congregation he had served. Lyle
was the first person to confront him with this
all-too-common pastoral situation. When Lyle gave
him the news, he "hemmed and hawed." He stood
first on one foot and then on the other. His mind
raced through every wise saying he knew. He
prayed God would fill his mouth with wise words,
cause him to disappear in a mist, or wake him from
this bad dream. He was a minister of the gospel of
Jesus Christ. Certainly there was something meaningful to say in this situation, but he had no idea
what it might be.

From his hospital bed, Lyle said what needed to
be said. "Bob, the news I gave you has obviously
upset you. You don't know what to say. I know
exactly how you feel. For years I called on the sick.
Many times I searched for words of wisdom.
Sometimes I thought the things I said were helpful.
At other times, I was not so sure. Now I am the one
in the bed with the bad news. I assure you nothing
needs to be said. You are here as a representative of
Christ's church. That says everything important.
Just knowing you care brings comfort."

It has been many years since that day. Pastor Bob
is still grateful to Lyle. He freed him from an
embarrassing situation and taught him an important principle of pastoral care: It is not necessary to
have a word from the Lord on every topic and in
every situation. Since that day, Pastor Bob has
searched many times for something wise, comfort-

ing, or inspiring to say. How glorious it is to have something significant to break the deafening silence of the hospital waiting room or the funeral home lounge. But with experience, he has learned to disguise the helplessness he felt at Lyle's bedside. He also learned a few things that are sometimes helpful to say. Mostly, he learned to accept that not much can be said.

There are times, of course, when the family expects the church's representative to be filled with wisdom. Attempts at meeting this expectation usually end in frustration. It is better to endure the quiet. After all, God is not mute in the midst of our silence. The voice of the ordained minister is not always needed.

Don't succumb to the temptation to be an "aginner"!

Pastor John never makes positive comments. In every clergy gathering, committee meeting, and denominational assembly, he finds something to complain about. Never content to keep his thoughts to himself, he grumbles a commentary for the benefit of those seated nearby. When they do not listen, he continues a monologue. He frequently monopolizes question-and-answer sessions with his views. He interrupts speakers during presentations. He corners group leaders to inform them why he does not agree. When an idea is suggested or a plan of action reported, John points out its problem or weakness. John is an "aginner." It does not matter what it is, he is against it.

This approach has benefits. Many believe John extremely intelligent and some find his analytical ability remarkable. Speakers prepare themselves well when he is present. They know they must respond to his complaining. John seems to enjoy his ability to steer group discussions toward himself. In doing so, however, he brings misery to those around him.

Actually, John is not particularly insightful. The created order has few perfect things. Every idea, plan, suggestion, person, and situation is flawed. Special abilities are not required to understand this nor does it take talent to complain about imperfections. Negatives can always be found, but those who choose to specialize in pointing out the obvious are often accorded the status of expert. Earning this designation does not require making positive comments or helpful suggestions. Being an aginner carries prestige without asking for contribution.

Some clergy succumb to the temptation of being aginners. They are difficult to befriend. Because they must be alert to imperfections, they never relax their fault-finding vigilance. Thus, they do not experience the blessedness of offering appreciation. To the aginner, living means cleaning out the barn without getting to ride the pony. While doing the dirty work, they never have any fun—a high price to pay for a few close friends who admire their analytical ability.

The world needs people who can see possibilities in spite of problems and are willing to emphasize positives in the face of negatives. The minister who resists the temptation to be an aginner is easier to be around, a more satisfied person, and a more effective pastor.

Weddings marry the romantic and funerals bury the dead—do not expect either to be effective tools for church growth.

Most ministers are periodically asked to function as community chaplain. If a family tells the funeral home director the deceased had no church affiliation (which means they cannot remember him attending a worship service within the last thirty years), a local pastor will be asked to conduct the funeral. Some ministers mistake this as an opportunity for church growth rather than a request for a simple act of kindness. Acting on that misunderstanding results in disappointment.

The family will be appropriately grateful. Some people even demonstrate their gratitude by attending worship a time or two. Seldom, however, does the relationship that begins with a funeral grow into a meaningful church affiliation. Wise pastors conduct funerals for non-church members as acts of kindness and not in hopes of gaining new members.

The same principle holds for conducting the weddings of the unchurched. Some clergy mistake the phone call that begins, "Do you do weddings for people who do not belong to your church?" as a query about membership. More typically, the caller is merely shopping for a religious building. In most cases the call to the church comes after clearing the reception for the American Legion Hall.

Be prepared for the worst when conducting weddings for the unchurched. Assume nothing. Seldom do these people understand elementary church etiquette. Place "No Smoking" signs in the sanctuary as well as in the rest rooms. Mention that the communion table is not to be used as an open bar. Prepare for the worst and rejoice when it does not happen. This will help prevent needless disappointment.

Someone suggests wise ministers think of weddings as the undeniable evidence of the grace of God. What other explanation can there be? A wedding frequently brings together two people with levels of passion infinitely higher than their knowledge of each other. Without proper skill or experience to hold it in place, she wrestles with a strapless dress. He wears a lavender tuxedo, pink ruffled shirt, and coordinated headband. The music comes from a movie about a juvenile delinquent who burns down his girl friend's home because he dislikes her father. And the guests hope the flower girl can control her bout with the flu long enough to get through the ceremony.

With infinite variation, this strange rite of passage starts society's most enduring institution and the instrument by which our greatest values are carried from generation to generation. Do not be surprised that so many marriages end in divorce. Rather rejoice that so many weddings lead to decades of happiness. Indeed weddings are demonstrations of grace.

Performing weddings and conducting funerals for unchurched people are the caring acts of a loving pastor. A funeral ministers to a grieving family. The most realistic goal for the wedding ceremony is minimal embarrassment for all concerned. Neither weddings nor funerals, however, should be thought of as effective methods of church growth.

If it works, don't fix it. In fact, you may not even want to ask how it works.

Upon arrival in a new ministry, it is wise to remind oneself: "This congregation operated before I came. It will probably operate after I leave. The people of this church already have ways of getting things done. I will not make changes until I am convinced the present ways do not work and neither the congregation nor I can exist without altering them."

Never assume the newsletter cannot be published, the committee meetings cannot be scheduled, the church cannot be cleaned or anything else cannot be completed by any other method than the one the minister proposes. These assumptions usually lead to one of two results: (1) irritable members are disturbed by what they deem unnecessary change or (2) the congregation may agree with the minister and relinquish responsibility for those functions. This adds unnecessarily to the pastor's workload. Either result leaves much to be desired.

Accept that there is more than one way to perform a function or solve a problem. The method the congregation currently uses may not be the best, especially true when "best" is defined as the way the minister thinks it should be done, but if it works, do not fix it. Standing aside and letting some things happen prevents pain, perspiration, and hassle. It also permits the minister time and energy to work on things that *need* fixing.

This principle is practiced when things regularly happen without the minister's knowledge. What joy comes in realizing, "I have no idea how volunteers are found for the Crib Room, how people are scheduled to clean the sanctuary, how it is determined which deacons serve the Lord's Supper, and I am not required to know."

Understand the difference between an incident and an issue.

When four-year-old Billy stomps angrily into the kitchen and declares, "I am going to kill Jimmy. He pushed me down," the wise parent realizes this is an *incident.* The child needs direction in more healthy ways to express his anger. It is not, however, necessary to alert the police or register Billy for three years of intensive psychotherapy.

On the other hand, if Billy is a forty-year-old Vietnam veteran with a history of violent behavior and makes the same announcement with a loaded pistol in his hand, it is a serious *issue.* Issues require more extensive responses than incidents because they are substantially more serious.

Although there is no simple method to discern issues from incidents in the pastorate, degree, frequency, and intensity are usually good indicators. One anonymous letter containing an unfavorable analysis of one's leadership probably indicates an incident. It does not mandate a career change to insurance sales. On the other hand, a unanimous resolution by the church board demanding the pastor be tarred, feathered, and run out of town on a rail indicates a serious issue. Learning to make this distinction and to respond appropriately to issues and incidents minimizes pastoral discomfort and enhances effectiveness.

Be aware of Bell's syndrome—the bane of a competent minister.

Unlike Murphy's Law, Bell's Syndrome is not among the widely known principles of human interaction. It was described only recently by Gail Bell, a friend and fellow pastor. Bell's Syndrome holds that *improved performance raises expectations.*

We regularly encounter this pattern. People evaluate the U.S. Postal Service by the standards of Bell's Syndrome. Every Third World traveler realizes what a good job the U.S. Postal Service does. We do not, however, want to compare our system to a developing nation's. We want to compare our system with the ideal: every piece of mail delivered correctly. We are not willing to settle for less. In fact, if that level of service is attained, we will establish an even higher one. The more something improves, the more improvement we demand. This drives expectations even higher and usually elicits criticism rather than praise. It is a human characteristic.

Bell's Syndrome also operates in the church. No matter how many young people are participating in the youth program, people will claim they know some who are not being reached. Church music programs never meet with everyone's approval. No matter how good, "It is still not the Mormon Tabernacle Choir." Every improvement in communicating the church's business and programs will be matched with a higher level of expectation. Eventually someone will note that on Air Force One, the President gets information faster and more accurately than the members of this church!

The congregation cannot be administered so that every member will offer the pastor uninterrupted praise. The wise, happy, and effective minister accommodates this unchangeable principle of human behavior. The alternative is to make the pastorate much more difficult than necessary.

BITES CAN BE MEANINGFUL BLESSINGS

Pastoral ministry requires hard work and is not always appreciated. Even though careful observance of the safety rules helps, every minister loses an occasional pound of flesh. This does not mean the pastorate should be shunned as a dangerous occupation. Every occupation has hazards and many are more difficult than ministry. Few, however, if any, can be as rewarding, not just in spite of, but because of hazards. The Suffering Servant passages of Isaiah are a marvelous reminder that, by faith, wholeness emerges from the hard times.

CHAPTER VII

BE PREPARED FOR WEEKLY PREACHING

During the summer between college and seminary, Ray preached at a small country church. In preparation for this first preaching experience, he worked the entire spring semester on his sermon. As the first Sunday approached, he worried only about length. Did he have too much material? He feared he might speak longer than the twenty minutes allocated.

He glanced at his watch as he concluded preaching. After four months preparation, his sermon lasted seven minutes. In that time, he shared nearly every religious view he held. He had no idea what he would say next week, let alone every Sunday for the rest of the summer.

Weekly preaching ranks among the pastoral ministry's greatest challenges. The unrelenting creative demands of sermon preparation never diminish and can never be neglected. Nearly every pastoral minister goes on "live" every Sunday morning with ten to thirty minutes of new material. Writing twenty-minute weekly sermons is comparable to writing a medium-sized book each year! Very few authors and screen writers lay claim to being that prolific.

Congregations typically hold preaching in high esteem. After all, from the laity's perspective, weekly sermons are a minister's moments of greatest visibility.

Due to this importance, the two criteria most pulpit committees establish for calling a new minister are whether he/she likes people and whether he/she can preach well. Preaching and leading worship are not only important to the congregation, they are demanding on the pastor. In spite of this, few homiletics professors successfully convey to seminarians how much energy preaching requires.

In many respects worship compares with opera as the ultimate expression of its discipline. Opera requires the coordination of instrumental and vocal music with elements of dance, dialogue, and directing. Conducting opera calls on every skill available to the musician. As the ecclesiastical equivalent, leading worship requires that the pastor coordinate nearly all the disciplines of ministry. One must have an eye for the overall yet attend to every detail. Sermon preparation depends on the disciplines of study and prayer. Sermons may offer anything and everything from Christian education to counseling for the troubled. Indeed, conducting worship demands as much skill and energy as conducting an opera.

Like the musical conductor, the preacher faces serious risk of failure. At the same time, even the possibility of approaching the standard set by past performance and performers affords abundant opportunities for the deepest satisfaction. The interfacing of risk and opportunity that is part of leading worship makes preaching an enormous emotional drain and an energizer of the human spirit.

As a talent given by a loving God to those called to ministry, preaching qualifies as a gift. Obviously some pastors have more than others, but all have the gift. It comes as a fringe benefit with a clear mind, an empowered faith, and vocal chords. Like any gift, however, it needs to be cultivated, sharpened, and polished. Gifted preachers, like gifted athletes, musicians, and writers, must work hard to develop their talent. A legend about one well-known preacher holds that he had the ability to outline his sermon on a paper napkin while having dinner on Saturday night. Perhaps he did that on rare occasion, but do not be fooled. No one regularly preaches meaningful sermons without preparation. The unusually gifted may never have to work *as* hard, but they still work hard. The talent to preach comes as a raw material and not as a finished product.

Fortunately, those who have less talent can improve. We may never be great, but with desire and hard work, at least we can enjoy the satisfaction of improving at this crucial part of pastoral ministry.

A CHECKLIST FOR A MEANINGFUL SERMON

To improve sermon quality, a systematic method must be devised and implemented. Those who love the people of God hold themselves to preaching consistently meaningful sermons.

Ask the following standard questions of every homily. The higher the sermon scores on this checklist, the better the sermon.

1. Is this sermon in understandable English?

The typical American congregation worships in English. We do not preach in Latin, and we do not read the Sunday morning Scripture lessons aloud in Greek or Hebrew. Few Americans understand those languages. In spite of this, some ministers insist on preaching in "academic" or "theologic." These are no less than foreign languages to the average person. How ironic that the same clergy who never offend people with sexist terminology may not hesitate to offend great numbers of people by using a form of English better reserved for the classroom than the sanctuary.

A college graduate with seminary training has little trouble confounding those with less education or no seminary training. Comprehensibility distinguishes the well-constructed sermon. Stating complex ideas in the language of the people requires intelligence and pastoral sensitivity. The most insensitive egghead can confuse people with five syllable words.

Even the most learned congregations appreciate clear, simple speech. A church of academicians comes to worship God, not to wrestle with a lecture. Expressing a significant idea understandably without resorting to the theological jargon of seminary coffee breaks brings joy to the congregation and satisfaction to the preacher.

Simple, straightforward English does not, however, mandate simplistic preaching. In fact oversimplifying insults the congregation's faith and intelligence. Realistic descriptions of the world cannot be reduced to slogans appropriate for bumper stickers. Doing so fails to take people's hurts seriously. Effective preaching plumbs the depths of issues in a language people speak and understand.

2. Does this sermon speak of God?

The young minister asked the bishop, "What should I preach about?" The bishop replied, "About God and about twenty minutes."

Although sermon length varies with denominational tradition, this old story points out the need to speak from a theological perspective. A talk appropriate for a Monday Kiwanis meeting almost always makes a poor Sunday sermon. An after dinner speech may deal with a sermon's topic, but not in the same way. Pleasing pep talks on positive attitudes and challenging discourses on social issues can be shaped into sermons. They are not sermons in and of themselves. A sermon must speak of the God revealed in Scripture.

3. Is this sermon biblical?

Christian preaching proclaims the kingdom of God revealed in Scripture. The authority of the Bible distinguishes the sermon from a local politician's speech and the schoolteacher's history lesson. Few people, if any, come to church to hear the minister expound on the latest personality theory or offer quasi-religious views on the American political scene. The average minister does not have a TV talk show host's communication skills or Monday Night Football's mass appeal. First and foremost we are proclaimers of Scripture. Our only significant message is rooted in the Christ revealed in the Bible. Without that, we have little worth saying.

4. Does the sermon reflect confidence in the Scripture?

Many clergy express more confidence in the trustworthiness of theologians, social commentators, and personality theorists than in Scripture. While modern sources are cited as unquestioned authorities, the Scripture must be demythologized, put into historical context, or if it says something contrary to what we want to believe, simply avoided. The preaching of the minister embarrassed by the Bible does little to build the congregation's faith.

Many ministers simply need to rethink the issue of scriptural authority. Too many pastors' growth processes stop with an introduction to the necessity of critical thinking. Ministers must distinguish the scholarly work of preparation from the material appropriate for a delivered sermon. For instance, sermon preparation may demythologize Genesis 2–3. One need not spend half the sermon doing it for the congregation. The preacher must be familiar with the scholarly questions about Pauline authorship of Ephesians but do not bore the congregation with them. Sermons help people cope with the pain and complexities of daily living. Yet this happens only when the minister accepts the Bible as a trustworthy source of help for daily living.

5. Does this sermon speak to the needs of those who hear it?

Pastor Frank preaches each week on a different Christian doctrine. His sermon manuscripts read like a catechism from the Middle Ages. As an articulate Fundamentalist, he wants his congregation to know and to accept his narrow interpretation of the faith. He may also be one of the few people on earth who enjoys a weekly diet of theological hairsplitting. His sermon topics address his needs, not those of the congregation.

To be faithful to our call, we must preach the kingdom of God. People hear the Good News best when its concerns intersect their needs. To accomplish this, we must scrupulously avoid riding pet hobby horses and overfocusing on our personal concerns. A series of four sermons on "More Effective Functional Committees" speaks to the pastor's anxiety and not to the congregation's hurts. If we feel compelled weekly to mention our concern over American involvement in Central America or our horror at unregulated abortion, our interests are probably being addressed more often than necessary.

In order to preach the possibilities of the kingdom of God while remaining sensitive to people, try listing the problems, pains, possibilities, shortcomings, and joys currently being faced in the congregation. After each entry, list which sermons speak to which issues. If some issues are continually addressed while others are neglected, you must work to widen the choice of sermon topics. Unless we intentionally address significant needs, we may neglect them.

Entire groups may even be neglected. How easy it is to address the congregation as if every one were the same age, lived in the same family situation, encountered similar work conditions, and experienced the same economic conditions. As he or she speaks to the needs, the sensitive pastor also speaks to the diversity of the people. Address this problem with a chart of inclusiveness. List the age, sex, family status, working and living situation for each member. Examine sermon content to ascertain if the diversity of the people is being addressed. Sermons should discuss the single life as well as marriage and family. One must speak to issues that concern retirees as well as to issues that concern families with teens. Responding to this challenge makes one's ministry more effective and more satisfying.

6. Does this sermon say anything worthwhile?

What a tough question! After spending hours preparing it, we desparately want to believe the sermon worthwhile. This is not always the case. One must be prepared to cast aside the manuscript that does not measure up. The grace for such a courageous act comes only to the pastor willing to face the consequences of admitting the importance of the sermon. It also requires that one finish sermon preparation before late Saturday night or early Sunday morning. The sermon must be ready early enough to be set aside to allow the minister to rethink if it does not measure up.

7. Can the point of the sermon be summarized in one sentence?

Sermons are intended to be humanizing. The spoken word has the power to set people free to be the full human beings God intends them to be. When the congregation does not know the point of the sermon, that will not likely occur. To be effective, the sermon must say something important clearly and not be merely a time filler between the call to worship and the benediction.

A single sentence summary does more than ensure that the homily says something important. It actually facilitates sermon preparation. Before outlining the various subpoints, write the sermon's main point at the top of the page. Let this sentence become the benchmark to help avoid the "let's meander into the middle of this topic and make observations for twenty minutes before the closing prayer" method of manuscript preparation.

8. Is this sermon properly illustrated?

Balancing sermon illustrations can be as difficult as standing an egg on end. Too many illustrations make the sermon a series of stories tied together with transitional sentences. This style can be interesting but not edifying. On the other hand, insufficient illustrations make sermons as interesting as test tones. A sermon is properly balanced when the stories clarify rather than replace or obscure ideas.

Make no mistake about it, however: illustrations are crucial. They show how significant theological ideas relate to real people in real situations. Without a few empowering stories, some people might never realize the sermon had a practical application.

Illustrations also provide the fringe benefit of making sermons memorable. Seldom does the congregant recall a well-polished theological gem from a past homily. More likely, he/she will only recall a story told to illustrate the point. What a delight it is, however, on those rare occasions when both the illustration and its application are recalled accurately.

9. Does this sermon have any good news?

Etymologically, the evangelist brought good news

from the battle front. The preacher now serves the evangelist's role. We are charged with bringing good news to those who desperately need to hear something that will help them make sense of their lives. Preaching professor Ron Allen stated that he believes the key questions of our age concern hope and community: "Will the future be fit to live in? Can we learn to live with one another?"[1] People in the pews long to hear some reassuring good news in answer to these crucial questions.

In addition, preachers need to resist the temptation to scold those who have not lived up to their potential or to the preachers' expectations. The congregants who need to be told of their sins also need to be reassured of the possibility of forgiveness. When angry with the people, we should close with a kind word. No matter how disappointing their behavior, we should offer a word of hope before the benediction. Constantly riding the congregation for the error of their collective ways may temporarily make the preacher feel good, but it destroys the relationship between the pastor and the people. A word of good news, however, builds strong relationships and causes the congregation to believe the preaching has vastly improved.

A CHECKLIST OF "DON'TS" FOR IMPROVED PREACHING

The quality of sermons can be raised by testing each against standard criteria. Preaching can also be improved by avoiding certain things.

---

1. Ronald Allen, associate professor of preaching at Christian Theological Seminary, Indianapolis, Indiana, gave these remarks at a meeting of the National Evangelistic Association of the Christian Church (Disciples of Christ) in its meeting prior to the General Assembly of the Church in August, 1985, in Des Moines, Iowa.

Don't tell self-aggrandizing stories.

A Sunday sermon should not sound like a Christmas letter publicizing the author's current achievements. The pastor who makes himself/herself the star of sermon illustrations has a serious self-identity problem. On the other hand, the congregation responds positively to personal stories in which ministers admit their human frailties. People appreciate knowing the pastor shares space with the laity on the same rocky highway. A kinship develops among those who know they must develop tools for coping with the fallibilities of the world.

Don't succumb to the temptation of "I'm agin it" preaching.

Ministers commonly take stands against issues. Many things can and should be opposed. Multitudes even enjoy listening to variations on "what is wrong with the world today." On the other hand, becoming a negative nattering nitpicker exacts a heavy toll from preacher and congregation.

Don't use the pulpit to frighten people into older ways of coping.

Resist the temptation to stir reminiscences of the good old days when everyone was a nice Christian and saying, "Ain't it awful most people are not like that any more!" Even though television evangelists raise millions of dollars preaching this nonsense, and unscrupulous politicians can frequently ensure their reelection with the message, the local church pastor must avoid the practice.

Even if things used to be better (which is debatable), people cannot return. Rather than irresponsibly frightening people, the pastor should help people find ways to cope victoriously today.

Don't take credit for what is not yours.

Plagiarism is a serious ethical breach of trust. Credit needs to be given. Laws must be observed. The congregation does not expect the local church minister to be the source of every theological idea and sermon illustration. Attempting to make it seem that way does not impress people but causes them to question the integrity of the pastor.

Don't give too much credit.

Giving too much credit gets in the way of the message. After all, a sermon should not sound like an oral term paper. Read what others have written on the topic, permit their thinking to help shape the sermon, and credit them for what they offer. Do not, however, forget that the congregation deserves to hear what their pastor thinks on the topic. People are much more likely to be influenced by their beloved pastor's thoughts than most comments from an unknown scholar.

Don't speak in a monotone.

Congregations sleep when the worship leader uses only a narrow range of the voice. Practice speaking with enough inflection variety to keep the folks interested. If the congregants want to hear a boring voice, they can call Time and Temperature and listen to the computer.

While a monotone induces drowsiness, old-fashioned oratory irritates the congregation. The rantings and ravings associated with this style have been rendered obsolete by modern broadcast technology. Today's congregations respond best to a sincere, enthusiastic, and conversational preaching style.

Videotape a sermon at least once annually. Watch carefully for meaningless gestures, lack of vocal variety, unnatural speech patterns, and other distracting habits. Weed them out. Don't let your preaching become little more than an array of distracting idiosyncrasies.

TWO IMPORTANT FACTORS IN PREACHING

1. Good preaching requires a meaningful spiritual life.

Pastoral ministry provides multiple opportunities to feel like a failure. The congregation seldom responds to our preaching as vigorously as hoped. Rarely does attendance reach the goal we think reasonable. Very few people really appreciate our ministry as much as we think appropriate. A pastor could find many reasons to spend considerable amounts of time wallowing in self-pity.

Only a profound sense of eternal purpose permits us to face our failings. A nodding acquaintance with the Creator will not suffice. To bring God's Word to bear on people's lives today we must be intimately familiar with both God and the people. Good preaching requires that a preacher have a growing, disciplined relationship with the loving Lord. If this is missing, the congregation flounders, and the pastor finds little joy in ministry. On the other hand, where the pastor has a growing spiritual life and the preaching prospers, the congregation is fed and the pastor is satisfied. Any goal to improve one's preaching must include a program for deepening one's spiritual life.

2. People expect something important to happen during worship.

We live in a fragmented world. Everyone from the family doctor to the auto mechanic refers all but the most routine cases to a specialist. Is it any wonder people cry out, "Where is the wholeness in our lives?"

When people come to church they want to hear a word of hope. They do not want to be entertained. They want to encounter the living Word that has the power to make their lives more satisfying. They long to hear that wholeness comes by faith in Christ Jesus.

Preaching the Good News has power to make positive changes in people's lives. The trustworthy gospel has a centuries-old track record of effectiveness. A pastor perceived as a person of integrity can make important things happen. We are, after all, sharers of the Good News that has sustained the people of God and will continue to do so. Never forget the possibility that the people may hear an authentic word of life from the stammering lips of a fellow struggler along the way.

CHAPTER VIII

DON'T BE TRAPPED BY SUCCESS

Highly motivated, extremely competent Pastor Burt accepted a call from the Church of Many Problems because it seemed a challenge worthy of his many skills. The church reeled from years of continual conflict. In a matter of months, worship attendance increased from an average of 160 to an average of 280, and giving nearly doubled. People reported feeling good about their church membership for the first time in many years.

Rather than rejoicing in this success, Burt resigned after three years because he believed he failed the church and himself. His goals were unmet. He expected worship attendance to average over three hundred and giving to triple. He despaired because there was not greater involvement in church programs—the fact that people were exhausted from years of conflict did not occur to him.

His extremely high expectations energized him to work harder and harder to try to accomplish what was not likely to happen. In succession, he blamed his incompetence, the unappreciative congregation, their long history of problems and lack of Christian commitment. He even began to consider the long-term effects of acid rain, the high sugar content of breakfast cereal, and fluoride in the local water supply. Those who strive for success but feel like failures do not think clearly.

Americans admire successful people. Generally speaking, we look up to those who have more and do more. We believe people with higher salaries, bigger homes, and more expensive cars should be held in higher esteem than those who demonstrate less tangible results. This achievement-oriented method of valuing people and events ought to be commended. It has resulted in a high standard of living.

The Calvinistic work ethic undergirds our understanding of what it takes to be a successful person. When generation after generation believes hard work brings advancement and advancement leads to satisfaction, progress inevitably follows. We really seem to believe that joy results from success and success results from doing more and getting more.

As products of our society, ministers frequently come to value and strive toward this achievement-defined success. Local church ministry does not, however, offer many opportunities to attain this standard. In business, successful people are upwardly mobile. They get regular promotions, bigger offices, and constantly growing pay checks. Pastoral ministry cannot match those opportunities. If a promotion constitutes a call to a larger congregation, one must prepare for few promotions. Because there are few larger congregations, some capable pastors spend their careers in congregations of essentially the same size. Ministry does not offer many promotions to something bigger. Clergy cannot compete in terms of salary either. By the standards of the business world, little variation exists in clergy income.

Ministry competes with the business world only in office size and furnishings. Most ministers have offices with walls, a door, desk, and even a high back office chair. The pastor's study frequently has a credenza and an extra chair. In the business world, only fourteenth floor vice presidents are provided such surroundings. On most other matters, however, pastoral ministry cannot compete.

CHASING THE BIGGER AND THE STILL MORE

Before lamenting our misfortune, we should note the hazards inherent in pursuing the bigger and the still more. This model seldom provides the joy it promises.

Dave, who owns and operates a construction business, can be considered successful. His large home and several-car garage proclaim his income. He has a community reputation for being a hard-driving businessman and his company has grown tremendously under his capable leadership. In fact, every year for more than a decade, the financial volume and profit of his business have increased significantly.

Far from enjoying his status, David suffers from depression. Only after several months in therapy did he realize that he had been brought down by his pursuit of success.

"The 'shrink' finally helped me understand I am my own worst enemy," David explained. "To be happy I thought I had to be successful and I believed that, in order to be successful, my business had to continue growing. Each year I needed more volume, more employees, and more contracts than last year. If I didn't grow, I felt like a failure. That definition of success destined me to feel like a failure."

"Obviously it is not possible to always do better," David continued. "Because I didn't want to face that, I worked harder and harder. The more I worked, the more money I made and the more I feared next year I wouldn't be able to do better than this year. I ran scared for so long I got depressed. I felt like a failure because I knew I couldn't continue to succeed."

Many repeat this story in their own lives and discover pursuing this brand of success inevitably ends in failure. We cannot continue to grow bigger and do better. Somewhere, at some time, people either maximize their potential or reach the outer limits of reasonable growth. When this happens, even the biggest and best believe themselves failures.

Although clergy seldom succumb completely to

this secular standard, we have our pastoral equivalents. Whenever clergy gather, bigger and better issues are raised. "How many additions did you have this year? How is worship attendance this Lent? Is your budget keeping up with inflation?" Conclaves of clergy, like meetings of managers, have a ritual by which we test the waters, evaluate the competition, mention personal achievements, and determine who the candidates might be for the next promotion, i.e., larger congregation searching for a pastor.

Despite theological inappropriateness, clergy frequently seek secular brands of success. We set measurable goals, strive to achieve them, and then set higher ones if we do. While having some value, it can also get out of hand. We frequently and mistakenly tie self-worth to achieving goals. We might even foolishly equate achieving growth goals with entering the kingdom of God.

A colleague lamented the poor stewardship and consequent budget problems of his church. He raised questions about the effectiveness of his leadership, and he wondered if he had accomplished all he could. Was it time to leave?

His sense of failure resulted more from striving for success than any actual financial or stewardship problem. Income was at the same level as last year in spite of the fact that there was one less Sunday for the same period. Giving was up 25 percent over three years ago. Rather than a cash flow problem, the church was nearly a year ahead on building fund payments and had a general fund checkbook balance of $25,000.

The problem was not a financial one; it was simply the fact that the pastor expected greater growth. Like Dave and his construction business goals, this pastor tied self-worth to continual growth. Obviously, every pastor needs to set stewardship goals and to work toward them. One must not, however, become obsessed with achieving them.

Pastoral ministry does not lend itself to the secular notions of success as more, bigger, and better. Congregations differ from corporations. Attempts to make ministry fit a purely business model seldom work. As mentioned, these forms of success do not even serve the business community well.

The pursuit of any unrealistic goal results in feeling like a failure. As generally idealistic people, clergy frequently have high expectations for themselves and the congregations they serve. Many even operate on the assumption that they will be able to solve all the problems of all the people in the church. Given the bold claim of the Christian faith that people can do more and be more by faith than they can ever do or be without faith, that idealism can be understood if not justified. In fact, idealism ranks as one of a pastor's greatest assets. It may, however, bring a considerable amount of pain. The pastor expecting to experience the ecstasy of being the perfect minister serving a perfect congregation will be disappointed. Striving to attain the unattainable results in despair.

People frequently enter full-time Christian service with heady dreams of idyllic nonsense. What a terrible shock to discover that human sinfulness permeates every aspect of church life. In fact, sinners have all the votes on the church board and seldom believe that they are as off-target as the pastor thinks they are.

When the pastor perceives this grim reality as a problem needing a solution, takes on every little issue as if it had to be solved rather than endured, idealism quickly turns to frustration which eventually leads to despair. Unrealistic expectations can have no other result.

A MORE FAITHFUL WAY TO SUCCESS

The pursuit of success becomes idolatrous when it functions as the central motivation for living. This does not mean, however, that we must abandon all hope of feeling successful. It only means we need to define and pursue a healthier, theologically appropriate understanding. After all, a better understanding of success can serve us as readily as an idolatrous one can consume us. Like all human beings, ministers want to avoid the anguish of failed attempts at success. We also want to be able to consider ourselves successful people. While not easy, we can walk this fine line.

1. Define success interpersonally.

In the 1960s and 1970s, the church became enamored by the management techniques of business and social service agencies. Churches attempted to operate by models that worked effectively elsewhere. The insights of community enablers and organizational development flooded the church. The operational flow chart of many middle judicatories and even local congregations still abound with terms such as "management team" and "task force."

While much of this has been helpful, some has been disastrous. Everything that works in business, government, and social service agencies cannot be adopted by the church. The church's primary concern remains the cure of souls, not management by objectives. When we are more concerned with meeting goals than caring for people, we have forgotten what it means to be the church.

It is, of course, important to keep measurable goals before the church. The church growth movement ably points to scriptural comments on the numbers of people joining the church. We deceive ourselves when we say we are concerned about people but fail to discuss numerical goals for the people we want to reach, the money we seek to raise, the programs we want to conduct, or the buildings we plan to build. Some of the techniques and insights from organizational development and business management also help build models for working with people. We must not, however, mistake ends for means. Ministerial success cannot be measured by the pastor's salary, the congregation's budget, the average worship attendance, or the evangelism record. The success of any congregation or pastor should be determined by what happens in the lives of those who are being touched by congregation and pastor.

Therefore, the construct success as a means of evaluating pastoral performance should be defined interpersonally. Does this pastor do well at meeting the needs of people, enabling them to grow in their faith, and awakening in them a sense of trust and security? These issues determine effectiveness and thus success in ministry.

Some obvious difficulties exist in assessing success by interpersonal criteria rather than ability to meet objective goals. If there were more people in worship this year than last, the congregation is growing. What measurement indicates whether or not the members of the congregation are growing in the sense of the presence of the living God? How does one measure if the congregation utilizes the teachings of the gospel as a basis for making ethical decisions more this year than last year?

Although impossible to measure scientifically, and even difficult to determine subjectively, the quality of ministerial performance can be evaluated.

(a) Record in a journal the contacts, conversations, visits, and events where you feel you have made a significant contribution in ministering to the needs of others. Jot down enough information to recall the incident later.

(b) Listen carefully for the comments, praise, and compliments others pass on to you. Most ministers receive far more praise than condemnation, but frequently listen only for complaints. Record every positive comment and refer to these entries later. Particularly on a bad day, great encouragement can be read into these accumulated "good words." Keep a file of "nice" thank-you notes and letters. Read them periodically as a reminder of the positive happenings which, frankly, dominate the experience of pastoral ministry. Immerse yourself in these positive comments and do not hesitate to think you are a success. It feels good.

(c) Use the latest pictorial directory or membership list as a guide for meditating about the contributions you regularly make to families in your parish. Reflect on the specific ministries you have offered. Pray for each family and plan pastoral care activities based on these prayers and meditations.

When one takes the time to think, reflect, meditate, and pray about the specific ways one has ministered and plans the ways one will continue to minister, rising feelings of self-esteem and success follow.

This activity can, of course, be taken too far. It could potentially become nothing more than the practice of pride. Ordinarily this does not happen. Experience indicates that the Almighty assigns at least one person in each congregation to keep the pastor humble. Competition for these positions must be stiff because so many who are "called" to the task are good at it.

2. Be an "expert" at something—in fact, at anything.

In the twelfth century, theology was queen of the sciences and the parish cleric was the community's most respected citizen. In that age, pastoral evaluation by interpersonal criteria was sufficient, but conditions have changed. Clergy live in a secular society, and this makes us all long to be successful in some measurable way. Therefore, effective ministers usually develop some skill in which they can excel.

Because the parish provides a flexible time schedule, ministers typically can become involved in everything from free-lance writing to raising roses and from coaching the local high school baseball team to developing expertise as an after-dinner speaker. Other ministers derive great joy from denominational and middle judicatory ministries. Still others engage in every activity from conducting evangelistic rallies to becoming the area expert on anything from Christian education to microcomputers to social justice issues. One can even specialize within pastoral ministry in anything from youth work to marriage counseling to geriatrics.

Every local pastor needs something at which to be

an achievement-defined, goal-oriented success. During those moments when one feels overwhelmed by parish responsibilities, what a source of joy to point to something concrete and say, "I am good at that. I am a success!" As long as the minister stops short of idolatry, he/she should pick a specialty and do it.

3. Take time to appreciate the journey.

Most satisfaction comes in pursuing rather than attaining goals. Therefore, one must learn the art of appreciating the journey rather than wait to arrive at the destination. A seminary education may only be a means to an end, but what a highly enjoyable means. Be intentional about finding ways to enjoy the basic preparation for ministry, the continuing education toward an advanced degree, and even the reading program one establishes to keep abreast.

Pastors frequently find themselves serving churches in communities far from the nation's intellectual and cultural centers. In some of these settings one gains a new appreciation for the adage: "The best thing about being here is that it is on the way to someplace else." Even the most isolated, backward community, however, offers certain lessons and experiences. Do not wish away your life and ministry, but enjoy these parts of your journey. Experience teaches that the next place will not differ greatly from the present one.

4. Do self-evaluations at longer intervals.

Weekly evaluations are built into pastoral ministry. The rhythm of parish life builds toward Sunday morning when the entire congregation expresses its opinion of the pastor's work by presence, absence, offerings, comments, and complaints. This puts a subtle and cumulative pressure on a pastor. Adding to the strain, most ministers tend to evaluate themselves and one another at least as often and frequently less forgivingly.

In the midst of constant evaluation, the tiniest variation can be experienced as catastrophic. The conscientious pastor may lose a night's sleep when attendance drops slightly for one Sunday. If it happens on two consecutive Sundays, despair may be the order of the week. When it happens on three Sundays in a row, the pastor may even consider making a move.

In all probability no problem exists. Short periods of reduced attendance can be explained by vacations, illness, bad weather, or the beginning of a periodic cycle of unexplainable Cannonball Sundays—so named for the ability to fire a cannonball down the center of the sanctuary without hurting a soul.

To avoid unnecessary despair, put greater distance between self-evaluations. Do not compare this week's attendance with a year ago this week. Instead, compare all of last year with all of this year. Limit the conversations with colleagues in which everyone tries to explain exactly how things are going right now, how they feel about it, and how they plan to improve it.

People who constantly think about the state of their health are called hypochondriacs. They make themselves sick. Constantly evaluating one's ministerial performance has a similar effect. While a little evaluation can be positive, too much makes you ill.

5. Learn what the possum has not seemed to learn.

When chased into a corner, this can be identified as a faith issue. Pastors who lose sight of the proper order of things become trapped by the pursuit of success. People are not the captains of their ships or masters of their fates. In the final analysis, we cannot do it all on our own. Fortunately, we do not have to. We are empowered by faith.

The person consumed by the search for success forgets this. Although frequently unexpressed, many people who despair over not feeling successful thought that if they worked hard, studied long, and exercised diligently, all things would work together for perfect goodness and the peace that passes all understanding.

Striving toward perfection may meet with initial success. Small accomplishments, however, lead to setting higher goals. Tiny accolades encourage ever-expanding objectives. The most talented, hard-working, and creative pastors may even experience several years of victory followed by success. After all, God calls many extremely able people to ministry. Rather than Yankee ingenuity, the grace of God should be credited.

Yet sooner or later the most creative person encounters a situation over which he/she has no control. The outer limits of human ability are reached and personal strength wanes. The talents and abilities that served a lifetime are found wanting. The reliance on self that once worked is no longer adequate.

The plight of the possum offers a good analogy. For tens of thousands of years, this ugly marsupial relied on "playing dead" to discourage enemies. Whenever frightened, the possum rolled over until the threat passed. For several thousand generations, this proved highly effective.

The method has serious weaknesses. For instance, "playing dead" magnifies the danger if used when crossing an interstate. In the same way, relying on personal ability may work well for long periods of time. It does not, however, always work. Everyone encounters a problem, challenge, or goal that is too big to handle. When this happens, we have to learn new ways. We have to accept our helplessness and utter inadequacy and rely on the strength God offers. Faith does not promise goal-oriented success. Instead, faith teaches that we are worthwhile simply because we are the children of God. Grace does not come by hard work or by meeting our goals. It comes as the free gift of a loving God.

When we understand and practice all these things, we can be successful without being trapped by success.

CHAPTER IX

TEND FAMILY, STUDY, FITNESS, AND THE SPIRITUAL LIFE

Imagine being assigned the task of preparing a well-balanced, one-dish meal for a large gathering. To successfully complete the task, of course, you must have the right ingredients prepared according to the recipe. The ingredients must be mixed in proper proportion, stirred thoroughly, and cooked together in one huge pot that covers all four burners. In order to cook the food evenly under these limiting circumstances, all four burners must be carefully adjusted. If some flames are properly tended and others neglected, the food will cook unevenly and improperly. Successful meal preparation requires that the burners be carefully adjusted and maintained.

We might look at pastoral ministry this way. The roles of prophet, priest, and wise ruler are analogous to the basic ingredients. Attitudes about success and busyness are the seasoning. Learning to deal with difficult people can be thought of as the necessary cooking skills. These ingredients, attitudes, and skills must then be "cooked" over four carefully tended "fires." These are the fires of physical fitness, spiritual life, family relationships, and personal study.

Maintaining these disciplines properly makes balancing the roles of office possible. Neglecting them ensures that they will never be balanced.

TEND TO HEALTH AND PHYSICAL FITNESS

"If you don't take care of your body, where are you going to live?"

This insightful, albeit folksy, question closes a local chiropractor's radio ad. It highlights the importance of maintaining this temple in which our personhood resides. No one has found a substitute residence for the personality. We should not, of course, mistakenly equate health for happiness. Unhealthy people can be happy. Poor health, however, makes it more difficult to appreciate life. The better your health, the easier it is to maintain a positive attitude, to accomplish more, and to have a more satisfying ministry.

Good health should not be taken for granted. It

cannot be maintained as naturally as falling asleep. Sustaining health requires a certain amount of effort. The healthiest people usually follow a program of diet and regular exercise.

These generalities apply to clergy as well as to the public at large. Job performance and satisfaction are directly related to health. If you are a good steward of your health, your ministry will more likely be effective and satisfying. Ministry, after all, cannot be disembodied. The weekly schedule of long days, pastoral care crises, frequent meetings, office counseling, administrative responsibility, home and hospital visitation added to the usual miscellany of studies, duties, and interruptions requires a healthy body as well as a positive attitude and a well-trained mind. Healthy bodies and healthy minds require intentional disciplining.

While clergy give intellectual assent to this fact, they still feel that physical fitness smacks of the fleshly, evil, and worldly. Sometimes we act as if the spiritual nature of ministry puts us beyond the mundane concerns of health and physical fitness.

On the other hand, we are busy people. Our reluctance to give priority to health and physical fitness may stem from practical concerns. In a ministerial association gathering, the conversation concerned the availability of group rates for ministers at the local health club. One indignant clergy said, "I don't believe the purpose of this organization is to make *recreational* opportunities available to the membership."

In making *recreational* sound like a four-letter word, she may have touched on the reason for which many clergy give a low priority to taking care of the body that houses the minister. We consider the pastoral task too important to interrupt for exercise and health care. Besides, practicing self-discipline at a church potluck dinner seems to cut at the heart of the covenant between pastor and congregation. Congregations tend to encourage gluttony as the clergy's only permissible sin.

We must confront these as mere rationalizations. We can facilitate our ministry by keeping our body as healthy as possible.

If health and fitness have been long neglected, some precautions must be observed. The overweight, underexercised body does not respond well when the fire of health and fitness is turned to fully on all at once. The minister who has not perspired since high school gym class should not begin with a five-mile run. Nor should one waste money responding to late night television advertisements about "guaranteed one hundred-pound weight loss in nine days—or we pay for the funeral!"

The pastor who has long neglected the body needs both motivation and a plan. Begin by being aware of the necessity. If you do not care for your body, there is, indeed, no other place to live. If you respond better to a theological rationale, remind yourself fitness involves the stewardship of a primary resource—physical life. Some of us can be motivated by first convincing ourselves that we have a professional responsibility to be as physically fit as possible. Taking better care of your cardiovascular system, after all, could extend a productive ministry ten years.

It needs to be mentioned, however, that these rationales serve only as an opening wedge. To be sustained, good health and fitness practices must become both fun and satisfying. Some clergy need to grow considerably before they are comfortable engaging in any activity "just for the fun of it." What a wonderful thing it can be when we eventually do that. Whatever you tell yourself, however, become convinced of this: You and your body are worth taking care of.

When you are aware of the necessity and motivated to do so, consult your physician. The doctor may or may not want to do a complete physical, but he/she knows how diet and exercise are likely to affect you. Do not risk making an erroneous assumption about the state of your health. Turning up any fire can be dangerous. Take precautions.

Consultations with physicians cost money. Not spending it, however, may be more costly. Ask the congregation to include money for a periodic physical examination in your salary/benefit package. This common practice of industry will be well worth imitating in the church.

Once your physician has ascertained your individual limitations and needs, develop a health and fitness program that is tailor-made for you. This may mean further consultation with a physician, hospital out-patient program, wellness center, YMCA, YWCA, or other agency that specializes in wholistic health planning and programming. You could be asked to take a computer scored test to assess the health risks of your life-style and personal history. You may need to undergo a fitness evaluation to measure your exercise capabilities, or you may need a diet or training program to change your eating habits.

Investigate available programs in your community. Remember, you are unique. Generic programs for diet and exercise may not work. Your needs and strengths must be assessed and a program must be developed especially for you.

Once you have a personal appraisal of your health risks, needs, and strengths, make a plan for doing something to improve and/or maintain your health. This may involve building on a strength or improving on a weakness.

Maintaining the fire of health and physical fitness requires effort. Fortunately, it does not take every ounce of resolve and strength. Watch your weight carefully, eat a balanced diet, engage in a regular exercise program and, by grace, the body will serve the minister for many years.

TEND THE CONCERNS OF FAMILY LIFE

While never a requirement, marriage remains a popular elective for Protestant ministers. When one chooses to have a spouse, one must be ready, however, to do the things that maximize the blessings and minimize the problems. The changing role of women and the greater number of two-career parsonage families make tending the concerns of family life both more difficult and more important. A troubled relationship at home makes an effective pastoral ministry much more difficult, if not impossible. On the other hand, a rich home life can facilitate pastoral ministry.

Among the common characteristics of long-lasting, joyful relationships, *commitment* ranks among the most important. Good marriages begin with a commitment to do whatever is necessary to accomplish that end. People who marry just to see if it will work discover it seldom does. After all, happiness is made, not discovered. Joy must be hammered out on the anvil of daily experience by those who commit themselves to finding a way to love one another.

Second, couples with long-lasting relationships have *realistic expectations.* Marriage has undergone a significant change in recent decades. For ten thousand years the family was society's basic unit of economic survival. In earlier centuries, people expected little more from their marriage than economic security. Today, however, economic necessity is one of the less important reasons for matrimony. Marriage has become society's basic unit of emotional security. A man does not choose his wife because she can help the horse pull a plow and a woman does not necessarily marry for financial support. Today, we expect marriage to support us emotionally. We expect a spouse to be a friend, a companion, and someone with whom to walk through the years.

In making this transition from an economic to an emotional motivation for marriage, our expectations are subject to becoming unreasonable. Some of us actually expect our mate to meet every emotional need at all times. Some couples want to settle for nothing less than a perfect relationship. When two people discover persistent human frailties in each other, they frequently abandon their marriage.

A couple with a marriage that sustains them, and enriches the ministry as well, knows how to keep marital expectations realistic. Because parsonage relationships are as imperfect as parishioner relationships, clergy and spouse need high motivations for working on problems and low expectations for solving all of them.

A third key to making a marriage work is *flexibility*. Couples with long-lasting relationships make adjustments for constant change in each other and in the marriage. People constantly change. Consequently the relationship must constantly change. Lasting relationships remain open to continuing reevaluation, renegotiation, and recommitment.

Obviously this requires that husband and wife spend time together. How much time will always be open for discussion, but there must be time to talk. People who do not take time to keep up on the events in one another's lives become strangers. Keeping a commitment to have time together may require a regular appointment on two busy schedules. If that is what it takes, do it. It will be worthwhile. No relationship can be flexible without the time to undergo some bending.

Fourth, *accentuate the positives and minimize the negatives*. Few if any marriages are strengthened by constant nitpicking. Most people require a constant supply of positive strokes. The writer of Proverbs reminds us, "Kind words are like dripping honey, sweetness on the tongue and health for the body" (Prov. 16:24 NEB). Whether in the giving or the receiving, positive, kind words strengthen and enrich our lives. Just as we need food each day, we need to say and to hear positive things.

Because every relationship has negatives, we cannot communicate only good things while avoiding all the bad things. Negatives, however, should be given in proper proportion. In the most mediocre relationship, there are ten things right for every problem. Communication within long-lasting relationships usually reflects that reality. The healthiest Couples are at least ten times more positive than negative.

Love is a fifth common ingredient in satisfying marriages. Married people best express their love for their spouses by being as concerned about their welfare and happiness as they are about the other's. Whenever possible—and loving people in marriages discover that is almost always—disagreements should be settled on a "win-win" basis. If either spouse has to give so much that he/she thinks he/she has lost, the relationship loses. When this happens, there are no victors.

Finally, the lasting relationship requires a shared and growing *faith*. Nothing else needs to be said about this essential ingredient for a satisfying relationship in both parsonage and non-parsonage families.

The well-tended fire of family life energizes ministry. When neglected, the home fire becomes one more dangerous house fire.

DO NOT NEGLECT THE INTELLECTUAL LIFE

While not an academic pursuit, pastoral ministry has an essential academic dimension. Study for ministry must continue throughout life. Skills must be updated constantly. Sermon preparation requires continued study. The minister's mind must be constantly fed to enrich the experience of living.

The condition of the pastor's library tells a great deal about his/her commitment to maintaining the fires of intellectual life. How sad it is when the only new books are compendiums of sermon illustrations, the theology shelf contains only seminary textbooks, and everything on biblical studies comes from Sunday school curricula. An outdated or incomplete library indicates that the minister operates on knowledge and skills that are no longer current. Such gross neglect of the intellectual life exacts a high price. When the fire goes out, the minister and the ministry suffer.

Although not as dangerous as total neglect, reading and studying *only* for sermon preparation has painful results. People who read only to find illustrations, topics, and titles for the Sunday morning homily intellectually wither. Good preaching comes from the overflow of ideas, illustrations, and the processed material from disciplined study. Sermons prepared by scraping the bottom of the barrel seldom edify a congregation or a preacher.

Law schools commonly teach future attorneys that only 20 percent of careful study can be revealed in the courtroom. Preaching should set the same standard; only 20 percent of the studied material should make the sermon manuscript. If everything you read and every point on which you reflect makes it into the sermon, your study has been sorely neglected. Poor study habits undermine ministry.

An effective, satisfying ministry depends on being a controlled yet compulsive consumer of information. A busy schedule permits little time for pleasure reading. Ministers must, however, learn to discipline themselves to find the time and choose carefully what to read. Those who simply do not like to read books, should take advantage of cassettes, videos, and magazines. A group of colleagues who meet regularly for study and discussion will also expand one's ability to grow intellectually.

There are a multitude of ways to maintain the fires of intellectual life. Develop an approach to personal study and follow it.

CAREFULLY TEND THE SPIRITUAL DISCIPLINES

Many laity believe that the typical minister spends at least two hours each day in prayer, Bible study, and meditation. How shocked they would be if they knew the truth. Pastoral routines are light years from the monastic life. Instead, the minister's Bible study may be limited to preparation for Sunday school lessons, prayers may be said primarily at hospital bedsides, and meditation may be practiced almost exclusively as a part of sermon preparation.

Too many pastors undervalue the spiritual disciplines. Sometimes they mistake sermon and worship service preparation for the serious attention to prayer and study needed for developing the life of the interiority. At other times, clergy come to the absurd conclusion that spiritual life needs no tending. In fact, a healthy spiritual life requires at least as much effort as disciplining the physical body.

Pastoral ministers desperately need a regular time and setting in which they may seriously practice the spiritual disciplines. Among other things, prayer, devotional study, and meditation provide opportunities for personal evaluation. The busyness of pastoral routine makes it difficult to integrate the meaning of events into an understanding of life. Without time to reflect, we race past moments of joy, forgiveness, reconciliation, and conversion without considering that these events have a transcendent dimension. When, in our unrelenting hurry to move from event to event, we do not periodically take time to evaluate what we believe, love, and value, we fail to grow intellectually or spiritually. Consequently, the quality of our life lessens. By not taking time to update our belief system by integrating events, we also miss the opportunity to help others reflect on the meaning of their lives. This diminishes the effectiveness of our ministry. A regular time for prayer and devotion addresses the problem.

A disciplined prayer life also makes us more empathetic. A people-intensive occupation like ministry makes emotional sclerosis a constant danger. We can become insensitive to the hurts in others. Taking time for prayer never exempts us from the warfare or provides a sanctimonious escape hatch from the struggle, sweat, and tears. It does, however, give us the opportunity to renew our strength and recenter our sensitivities.

Prayer and meditation rekindle the imagination, enlarge the vision, sensitize the conscience, stir the heart, enlist the will, and replenish the reservoir of compassion. An active, well-disciplined spiritual life makes an ordinary life extraordinary. Practice of the spiritual disciplines helps commonplace events flow with the living presence of God.

The rewards for tending the fire of spiritual life are significant and the cost of neglect is high. As with physical and intellectual needs, there are a multitude of ways to satisfy the needs of the spiritual life.

It will take a considerable amount of experimentation to determine the best way to maintain your spiritual life. Start searching. This fire, like the others, must be carefully tended and balanced with the pastoral, prophetic, and administrative duties of office. In fact, balancing ministry's ever shifting demands can be one of the most important tasks for minimizing misery and maximizing effectiveness.

CHAPTER X

SATISFACTION IS MADE,
NOT DISCOVERED

The person who permits the canoe to drift downstream invites disaster. Instead of arriving at the desired destination, drifting canoes run aground on sandbars, overturn on hidden rocks, and terrify passengers by passing beneath low lying branches. Only as one paddles the canoe faster than the current moves does one gain control over the direction the craft takes.

As with canoeing, the satisfaction resulting from

doing the ministerial job effectively does not result from an unplanned, unintentional, "drifting" approach to the pastorate. The hazards imbedded in the nature of our society and the church make it impossible.

Because satisfaction seldom results from a serendipity, few people accidentally stumble into the right combination of circumstances that guarantee they will live happily ever after. Ministers must accept the fact that there are no calls to a perfect congregation in a perfect community. Rather than being a matter of good luck, satisfaction in ministry results from planning, hard work, and a willingness to do the things that most likely bring satisfaction and minimize frustration.

In spite of the fact that happiness is made, not discovered, many people continue to wander from one congregation to another hoping one day everything will fall into place. They continue to search for the secret door leading to Utopia. They assume that if and when they find it, they can enter in and everything will be sweetness and light for the rest of their days.

Floating through ministry usually results in the ecclesiastical equivalent of being swept overboard by a low lying branch, running aground on a sandbar, or being overturned by an unseen obstacle. They may not have learned it in seminary, but effective ministers know how to plan for these obstacles to satisfaction.

RAPID CHANGE AS A BARRIER

In the play *Green Pastures,* one of the characters says, "Everything nailed down is coming loose."

This aptly describes how the winds of change blow at hurricane force. Unsecured clergy risk being blown about like so many unweighted empty trash cans on the courthouse lawn.

Persons ordained thirty years ago began ministry in a different environment. They did not have to be concerned with the ethical implications of heart transplants, contraceptive pills, moon landings, test tube babies, encounter groups, OPEC, TM, TA, SST, ICBM, Star Wars technology, terrorist suicide squads, or AIDS. These things did not exist. A thought was not given for the revolution in sexual freedom, the human induced breakdown in the environment, and the impending energy shortage. These crucial issues emerged later. Now each of them affects those to whom we are called to be instruments of God's love.

We must account for these technical and cultural changes by making certain they do not swamp the ministry or the emotional health of the minister. This will not be accomplished by drifting from one year to the next or from one congregation to the next. Effective ministers are aware of rapid and constant changes.

OTHER BARRIERS TO SATISFACTION

Some peculiarities inherent in the nature of congregational life also constitute barriers. For instance, many clergy run aground attempting to live up to the expectations of well-intentioned brothers and sisters in Christ. Pierce Harris, a United Methodist minister, observes, "The modern preacher has to make as many visits as a country doctor, shake as many hands as a politician, prepare as many briefs as a lawyer, and see as many people as a specialist. He has to be as good an executive as the president of a university, as good a financier as a bank president; and in the midst of it all, he has to be so good a diplomat that he could umpire a baseball game between the Knights of Columbus and the Ku Klux Klan."[1]

Would that it be that simple! Even if this could be accomplished, some folks would still not be satisfied. One group would disapprove of associating with the racist Klan and another of mingling with Catholics. Neither the Klan nor the Roman Catholic Church strongly support the Women's Movement. That would raise the ire of several. The advocates of a more peaceful life-style would criticize the pastor for participating in a competitive game like baseball. At least one person would be distressed that the pastor did not spend the time visiting a nursing home. The demands made by the typical congregation preclude finding real joy in ministry by simply drifting along hoping all will go well. One must carefully avoid running aground or being swamped by the over-whelming expectations of the congregation.

Trying to please all the people all the time is another dimension of this obstacle. It cannot be regularly done. In fact, only on rare, short-lived occasions can an entire congregation be pleased. A certain congregation's church board minutes had the following entry: "Elder Smith moved and Deacon Brown seconded that we hire Rev. Johnson as our next pastor. He is musically trained and has a history of outstanding youth work. What this

---

1. Marshall Shelley, "The Problems of Battered Pastors," *Christianity Today,* May 17, 1985, pp. 35-36.

congregation needs is a better music program and more youth work."

Two years later an entry in the official record of the church read: "Deacon Brown moved and Elder Smith seconded the motion that we fire Rev. Johnson. All we do in worship is sing and listen to the choir. He spends so much time with the kids, he neglects his calling on the elderly."

The Rev. Johnson experienced what the Master meant when he commented on how people criticized John the Baptist for his ascetic behavior and him because he was not ascetic enough. No matter what we do, someone disapproves. Criticism comes even to the minister who fulfills every congregational request.

The congregation in general never asks the pastor to be all things to all people. Collectively the church knows that cannot be done. Unfortunately, the pastor does not relate to the church collectively. Relationships come in individual units. Individuals often expect the pastor to be all things to them and their families, regardless of the conflicting demands. The family with teenagers desires a good youth program. At the same time, older members expect sound programming for Senior Citizens. While one group realizes the minister must spend considerable time oiling the ecclesiastical machinery, another group believes the pastor should get out of the office and into people's homes.

Any minister expecting to be all things to all people will discover it cannot be done. It anticipates the impossible. Striving to be all things to all people destabilizes the most stable personality.

Being held to a different set of behavioral standards magnifies the obstacles to satisfaction inherent in the clergy/congregation relationship. Ministers, quite frankly, are expected to do better than other Christians. The present generation did not, however, introduce this practice.

Sixteen hundred years ago, in *On the Priesthood* St. John Chrysostom noted:

> The minister's shortcomings simply cannot be concealed. Contrary, even the most trivial soon get known . . . however trifling the offences, these little things seem great to others, since everyone measures sin, not by the size of the offence, but by the standing of the sinner. . . . As long as the minister's life is well regulated in every particular point [all may remain well.] But if he [or she] should overlook some small detail, as is likely for a human being on his [or her] journey across the devious ocean of this life . . . that small offense casts a shadow all over the rest of his [or her] life. Everyone wants to judge the minister, not as one clothed in flesh, not as one possessing a human nature, but as an angel, exempt from the frailty of others.

While frustrating, effective ministers know to prepare for this reality. To drift along pretending it does not exist only invites disaster.

INTENTIONALLY SEEK SATISFACTION

Clergy are not alone in the need to intentionally pursue work effectiveness and satisfaction. The shelves of commercial book stores abound with best sellers on how other professions identify and handle this problem. In the business world those who drift along become the "burnouts." Sports broadcasters talk about the athlete who has "lost the edge." Who

among us has not encountered the teacher who
complains of a "lack of enthusiasm for the task"?
Still others refer to those who fail to intentionally
pursue effectiveness and satisfaction as having a
"lack of creative initiative." Regardless of the
profession, the job can be done effectively and
meaningfully only by those who are intentional in
their efforts.

THE FACT MUST BE FACED

Pastors choose what to believe about misery and
satisfaction. On the basis of what they believe, they
formulate a plan of action. Those who rely on
floating along hope to find the congregation and
community that will make them happy. Those who
believe misery is inevitable usually act in ways to
ensure that misery will come.

On the other hand, we are free to believe pastoral
ministry can and even should be satisfying. When
troubled, we can accept responsibility to make the
changes that will lead to greater satisfaction. While
believing it possible does not ensure it will happen, it
does open opportunities that are otherwise closed.

As the children of a loving God, we are not
relegated to existing as victims of circumstances
beyond our control. In spite of our obvious
limitations, we have a say in determining the
direction of our lives. When we decide our
ministries are going to be troubled, they will be.
When we decide we are endowed with certain
powers of positive self-determination, we open the
way to other possibilities. Indeed, as Abraham
Lincoln said, "People are about as happy as they
make up their minds to be."

DO YOU WANT TO BE HEALED?

One day Jesus was walking near the pool of Bethzatha. The area was crowded. People were waiting for the water to bubble. They believed the first into the stirring water could be healed of any infirmity. When the water moved, the sick made a mad dash toward the pool.

One man cried out to the Master for assistance. The pathetic fellow had been ill for thirty-eight years. He wanted the Master to help him be the first into the water. When Jesus heard his plea, he asked a curious question, "Do you want to be healed?"

We tend to think, "Why, of course, he wanted to be healed. Why else would he go daily to the pool? Why would he ask the Master for help?" On closer examination, the question makes sense. If the man was such a regular at the healing pool, why had he never found a way to be first into the water?

Perhaps he discovered advantages in remaining a cripple. Sympathy abounds. While not profitable, begging curtails the demand for hard work. What a marvelous social life. Sitting around the pool chatting with friends beats accepting responsibility for one's health, behavior, and happiness.

Clergy must ask themselves, "Do we want to be healed?" When we do not want to be healed, we continue to wallow in self-pity and blame our plight on society, the congregation, and other circumstances beyond our control. When we say we really want to feel better about doing ministry, we accept responsibility to work for changes that have a positive impact not only on our job performance, but on our own emotional health and well-being.

Those who do this understand the lesson that satisfaction is made, not discovered.

This is not an easy commitment. It requires giving up the good strokes of self-pity. No longer can we engage in mutual commiseration with colleagues. When we really want to be healed, we cannot enjoy the luxury of blaming the condition of our health or performance on other people and circumstances. We don't get to play the game of "Oh woe, ain't it awful." To say, "Yes, Lord, I really want to be healed" takes significant commitment.

A CONCLUDING COMMENT

These ten chapters outline the most important principles that lead to a satisfying and effective ministry. No claim can be made for originality. The less experienced pastor may not be familiar with all of them, but they are not secrets. Rather than rare insights, they are offered as gentle reminders of what it takes to make it in this extremely demanding, yet enormously rewarding calling and profession called pastoral ministry.

The following puts the work and joys of the local church minister very succinctly.

Being a minister means:
. . . spending three years studying systematic theology only to discover the most scholarly comment people respond to is "God loves you."
. . . never having enough money to pay one's bills nor enough time to count one's blessing.
. . . receiving two anonymous letters the same week. One written to correct the grammar in last Sunday's sermon. The other containing money for a family in need.

. . . seldom living near relatives, but always near friends.

. . . trying not to laugh when asked to say a blessing over the town's new sewage treatment plant.

. . . always working overtime, but seldom feeling the need to watch the clock.

. . . uniting with God's children at all the turning points of life.

. . . sharing the joys at the wedding and the tears in the hospital and funeral home.

. . . pushing the button of hope for those whose life has hit bottom.[2]

2. From a pamphlet of the Pension Fund of the Christian Church (Disciples of Christ) for the Week of the Ministry, 1974, by R. Robert Cueni. Used by permission.